Copyright © 2020 by Williams Commerce

All rights reserved. No part of this publication may be reproduced, distributed, or transmitted in any form or by any means, including photocopying, recording, or other electronic or mechanical methods, without the prior written permission of the author or publisher, except in the case of brief quotations embodied in critical reviews and certain other non-commercial uses permitted by copyright law. For permission requests regarding this story, contact the author or publisher.

Printed in the United States of America.

First Printing, 2020

<u>Publisher</u>
Williams Commerce, LLC

Williamscommerce1.com

ISBN: 978-0578736235

<u>Author</u>
Non-Profit Organization: Patrice's Kids

Patriceskids.com

Dedication & Acknowledgements

Opening up to the world and sharing my story was a painful process, but pain is a pre-requisite for healing. I wrote this book because there are so many children and survivors suffering in silence and the pain in my heart propelled me to be a voice for the voiceless.

It's heart-shattering that our laws haven't caught up to the damage that sexual abuse causes. By sharing my story, maybe, just maybe I can educate a parent about the damage that giving up on your child causes. Many parents chalk up their children's problems to misbehavior. However, I recommend digging deeper to find out what the problem is. You might just be surprised upon hearing what your child is struggling with. Children shouldn't fear their parents. They should be comfortable enough to tell you anything that may be bothering them. I dedicate this book to every single child going through abuse. You are precious no matter what anyone says.

I would like to thank the Brooklyn Veterans Hospital. I would not be where I am without all of their love and support over these years.

To Jason Soto: You may not know this, but you helped keep a smile on my face at work every day. I would be so down and depressed, and you would always come around with a joke or something positive to say to lift my spirits.

To Winston Chapman: You were the positive male figure that I needed in my life. You picked me up off the streets literally and helped give me a brand new start. You stuck by my side, and you never gave up on me.

To Brian: You know me more than anyone. All of those late nights crying on the phone with you and laughing. You visited me every time I was hospitalized. You were always there for me and had my back. We argue a lot, but at the end of the day I know who you are. Love you Bro!

To Jacob York: I told you my story, and you believed me, that means everything to me. You were the first person to speak on my behalf. I will always love you.

When I first decided that I was ready to write this book about my life. I had no idea where to start. The saying is, "Nothing is a coincidence in life." I met Ross Williams on social media and was immediately drawn to his page. He wrote two bestsellers in eight months. I did further research to learn he also owns a publishing and writing services company. I reached out to him, and the rest was history. Thank you so much for motivating me not to give up, but to keep writing because my story needed to be told. I would like to thank you and your company for providing me with services to help complete this book and for being such a kind soul with good intentions.

Super-talented Kel Fonville, you are a genius. Your illustrative work on my book helped to tell my story. You surpassed all my expectations and then took it a step further. I'm so honored to have you as a part of this project. Your work made everything come to life. You embodied my personality, my strength, and weaknesses through your artwork. Thank you so very much for all of your hard work and dedication. I look forward to working with you again. You are one of a kind.

Disclaimer

The Unconscious Community, which is authored by Patrice Griffin, details actual events of her life story. However, the characters names in the novel has been changed for legal reasons relating to the real life events. The selected names have no implications or insinuations of the real life names.

Table of Contents

Chapter 1 What The Fuck Am I Doing On This Train? 1

Chapter 2 Trouble Brewing 11

Chapter 3 Sliced 15

Chapter 4 There is an order 17

Chapter 5 Get Out 23

Chapter 6 Seven 28

Chapter 7 Weedie, Stop 33

Chapter 8 You Must Be Kidding 39

Chapter 9 Don't Forget What I Said 45

Chapter 10 Are We Clear? 53

Chapter 11 Enchanting 57

Chapter 12 Marathon 63

Chapter 13 Where Is Your Coat 66

Chapter 14 Paranoia 78

Chapter 15 My Best Option 89

Chapter 16 Pure Survival 95

Chapter 17 Sister, Mother, Niece 99

Chapter 18 I Remember You Sister 118

Chapter 19 A Battle Every Day 122

Chapter 20 My Voice 125

Chapter 21 Unconscious Community 133

Epilogue 135

Chapter 1 What The Fuck Am I Doing On This Train?

Damn, family. In my wildest dream as a child, I could have never predicted the reality of my teenage and early adult years. Being the golden child of my family appeared to be my peak in life, while I consistently experienced the unthinkable on a daily basis. As bad as I want to share my ultimate lows with you immediately, it's a must that I take you back to the beginning of my journey to show you and your loved ones how to avoid such pitfalls and tragedies. Sometimes we become armed with knowledge and experiences to become a vessel for others.

My journey started on a historically hot day in Brooklyn, New York. I was born on the 18th day of September 1975. Most of my early conscious memories consisted of being around my family. We were a tight-knit group that was entrenched in the Big Apple decades before my birth. I was born into a dual-parent household with my oldest brother, who is ten months older than me.

Alone time was an anomaly during my early childhood. Several of my aunts, uncles, and cousins lived on the same boulevard. I appreciated their close presence. However, nothing compared to having my favorite person in the world across the street from me. Thelma Collins, my maternal grandmother, was the most beautiful person in the world. She was beautiful on the inside and out. Many people that weren't even related to us felt the same way.

People gravitated to her in the neighborhood as if she were a member of the New York Knicks or Yankees. Both teams are arguably the most historic franchises in their respective sports. I could hear her heavy Barbados accent even when she wasn't in my sight. My grandmother moved from Barbados to the United States at the tender age of 11 to pursue a better life. She carved one out by becoming a nurse. A nursing salary wasn't enough for her family dynamics, which included being a single mother of twelve kids, so she had to create other streams of income.

Part of her popularity was due to becoming the first black woman who owned a barbershop in Flatbush, Brooklyn. She may have provided the best light fades in the entire borough. Even though she balanced both hustles, she still made time for her whole family. Most people called her mama, and she was my best friend. I was also close to my mom's baby sister,

Aunt Judy. I loved hanging with her. She would take me in the mornings to go and get bagels and hot chocolate. Aunt Judy had a huge influence on me growing up. She was so cool, artsy, and went down her own path from being a vegetarian to locking her hair and expanding her spirituality.

During my Kindergarten year, I spent most afternoons with my cousins. A lot of us went to the same school, so our friendships were closer than typical relatives. The innocence of childhood clouded my first few years of grade school. Everything was copacetic and normal until I returned home on a stormy day during my third-grade year.

When I walked through the door, a surprise was waiting for me at the kitchen table. Typically, I beat my father home, and my mother usually laid across the sofa watching her shows. When they were on, people knew to walk lightly. However, her shows were being televised, but the television was off. My father was rarely home when I returned from school, but he was sitting next to my mother that afternoon. Their presence threw my energy off, and I stopped in my tracks after I crossed the threshold. My dad signaled for me to take a seat, so I hurried to the table. After I sat down, he said, "Weedie, your mother and I have been talking about this for several months, but we concluded that its best we move to another part of town." Due to my young age, I don't remember my response verbatim. Once I conceptualized that I wouldn't be seeing my grandmother every day, I needed immediate consoling.

The following Monday, we moved to another neighborhood in New York that is better known as Bedstuy. It was an obvious economic upgrade, so I quickly developed an understanding of my parent's decision. My block was one of the safer places in Brooklyn. We had a block association president, and we respected our elders. If we didn't, we knew there would be severe repercussions from our parents.

None of the children my age were allowed to leave the block. I fantasized about being able to listen to the raps of Run DMC, Eric B, Rakim, and other New York rappers like most of the other kids. However, listening to rap wasn't allowed in my strict Christian household.

It was truly a blessing to have a brother so close in age. Miles and I shared several relationship qualities as twins without mirroring facial features. His friends were my friends, and my friends were his friends. A young boy by the name of

Chris Rock, who would become an internationally known comedian, also lived on my block. My Godmother also lived in the area. Although I enjoyed her company, my biggest motivation to visit her house was to pick off her blueberry tree. As cool as my new surroundings were, I still missed my old block. I missed my other family a lot, and I'm sure I didn't want to move, but I was too young to articulate that.

At the age of 8, my dad began acting funny around me like I was a burden to him. He intimidated me and terrified me. My mom went out often, and my dad stayed behind. It was like his sole intent was to terrorize me. One night while my mother was out on the town, he stayed behind to clean out the storage closet. It was packed to near capacity, so I helped him clean it out. My dad found two dead mice behind everything and began chasing me around the house with them. I don't remember how I escaped his wrath, but I remember crying myself to sleep that night underneath my bed with my favorite doll, Wendy. I couldn't wait until my mom got home because I thought she could save me, but I was sadly mistaken.

As I grew distant from my immediate family, I started growing closer to my cousin Lisa. She was a Pastor's daughter. Her mother, who was my aunt, pastored an Apostolic church a few blocks away from where I lived. They resided in an eight-bedroom mansion, which had plenty of space for hide-and-seek.

Lisa was five years older than me. She was the big sister I never had. Playing doctor and hide-and-seek were our favorite games. Our slumber parties went smoothly until the fifth one. It was a protocol for us to sleep in the same bed. As I was falling asleep, a cold hand rubbed up against my leg. Once I tried to move away, she got on top of me. Within seconds, I felt her heavy breaths in my face, and she began telling me how pretty I was. All my senses shut down until she tried to stick a thermometer in my anal. Lisa had a rebuttal for every cry of resistance and threatened me not to tell anyone. She made it seem like I would get in trouble for telling someone, and I felt at her mercy. I tried my best to open up about it, but I failed. How do you tell your parents something of that nature when one can't stand you, and the other one seems like they are in their own world?

Being molested by my own cousin played a major factor in my grades slipping. No one took heed to the change in my demeanor, and I felt invisible. The neglect caused me to slip in all areas of my life. I felt completely defeated once my parents got me a math tutor who gave me lessons at Lisa's house.

He was an older white male with a cheesy comb-over who smelled like pencils. We would be alone in the kitchen for two hours, three times a week. He started touching me on my shoulders first, and then his hands went in my shirt to rub my chest.

I grew accustomed to blocking out so much because of the trauma. He continued molesting me, and I remained silent about it as well. It was safe to say that my life unsafely changed for the worst. My trauma was replayed and recreated consistently. My dad's lack of nurturing played a major contributor to my low self-esteem and high self-hatred. I honestly felt like my mom was in a cloud and didn't bother getting to know me.

One memorable Saturday afternoon, my aunt's church had a block party service. The streets were closed due to the packed crowd, and my dad thought I left the block without permission. While I was behaving and hanging with my friends, my dad stormed towards my direction. Once he got within arm's reach, he cocked back and smacked me with all of his might in front of 200+ people. The sound of my father's hand that swallowed the average size hand, connecting with my face, sent chills through the onlookers. Although I mostly only heard my ears ringing, I could hear the crowd sympathizing, yelling, and crying.

I ran into the church as fast as my legs allowed me to. I was so traumatized that I urinated on myself. My friends came to check on me, but I was too busy crying my heart out to acknowledge them. To save face, my dad offered me a dry apology like he didn't do anything wrong. Instead of taking me home, he made me sit through the entire service in embarrassment and urine. Where was my mom during this, you ask? Your guess is better than mine. I don't think my mom was too fond of children. She tolerated us instead of loving us.

I hadn't seen my aunt Judy for a while, but one day she stopped by the house. I was so happy to see her. She came by to braid my hair. Shortly after aunt Judy started, she began telling me all about why I should not eat pork. She said it was one of the filthiest animals, and that was all I needed to hear. If she said it, then it was the bible. I never touched pork again. She had the most beautiful locks, and I wanted my hair just like hers. My mom was using the hot comb, but I was always getting burned, so we moved to weave ponytails. Eventually, Jerri Curls became popular. Everybody was rocking the curls, so I figured I would try it. Plus, it grew people's hair long. I wanted my hair to grow, so my aunt put one in my hair, and it lasted for a couple of days. Then all my hair fell out, and I was devastated.

Apparently, I had a sensitive scalp, and it didn't agree with the product. My mom had to give me a really short afro that resembled a meatball. I hated it so much. The kids in school were calling me bald-headed. It was the worst year for me. I was 11 when my hair grew back. When it did, I asked my mom if I could lock my hair like my aunt Judy since it was all-natural and gorgeous. She said she would think about it. I loved it when my aunt corn braided my hair or gave me box braids. The beautiful outcome made me disregard the pain from my tender scalp.

Finally, after weeks of nagging my mom, she told me, "If you want the locks, you can have them." During the late 80s, locks were not popular, but I didn't care because I wanted to look just like my aunt. She came over one Saturday morning with her jar of beeswax and hair grease to twist my hair. It took about an hour, and I thought it would look like hers, but she explained to me that it takes time for the hair to lock. Give it a couple of months, she said. The key is to wash your hair once a month.

Chapter 2 Trouble Brewing

I went several years without saying a word about the molestations. They persisted until shortly after my 12th birthday. Shortly after I turned twelve, my cousin Lisa said we couldn't do this anymore. Her reason was that God didn't agree, and she didn't want to go to hell. I was thankful for her "Coming to Jesus" moment. The tutoring sessions were also over.

Even though things appeared to be getting better, I felt trouble brewing. My dad started coming home late from work. He and his brother painted and built bridges for a living. We weren't rich, but we were well taken care of. One night my brother and I started hearing loud voices coming from our parents' room. My mom raised her voice and asked, "Where is our money that we are saving for a house?" He had been siphoning money from the account and left us penniless.

My father was smoking crack and cheating on my mom with a crackhead. This came as a complete shock to everyone. This bitch had the nerve to call our house, asking to speak to my mom. My mom spent a lot of time in her room crying. I knew it, and my brother knew. We didn't want her to cry, but secretly inside, I was happy.

Luckily for us, we had an enormous family that was very supportive, and we never went hungry or became homeless. It took everything in my mom to put her pride aside and get on food stamps.

Most people aren't the nicest when you're asking for help, but my mom's 11 siblings and mother helped us. One day after school, I was in my room doing homework, and I heard my mom and dad going at it. She packed his clothes and threw them down the stairs. Not even an hour later, his crackhead girlfriend showed up yelling my dad's name at the top of her lungs. I looked out the window, and I saw this Hispanic woman who looked strung out, repeatedly calling his name.

Instead of my dad telling the woman outside to leave, he went outside to entertain her. This was embarrassing for my mom. How the fuck could he hurt my mom like that? I knew he hated my guts, but him hurting my mom made it even worse. It was something I took personally. After all, she was all I had. My aunts and uncles got wind of the situation, and they handled it. She never came back, and my dad left.

My brother and I watched the whole situation from my mom's bedroom window. I was so happy that he left that I could have done a backflip without a running start. My brother was also happy, but mom was visibly depressed for a while. She had three kids, no job, and food stamps. However, my mom was a survivor, so she went to school and did what she had to do. Eventually, she landed an outstanding job at Pfizer pharmaceuticals.

My dad showed up months later on the steps of our house. My mom muttered, "Go downstairs, your father is here." He was gone so long that we changed his name to low down Harry. I sat on the steps, and he smelt funny, like a burnt smell.

Once I noticed bite marks on his face, I asked, "What happened?" He responded, "A rat bit me." I instantly felt sympathetic. He was living on an abandoned boulevard with rats. I know now that it was a crackhouse. I couldn't believe that I felt sorry for the same man that terrorized me as a kid. After our conversation was over, he handed me a wad of twenties and said, "Give this to your mother." That was the last I saw of him for a few years.

Chapter 3 Sliced

Middle school was one of the most challenging periods of my life. I was continuously called ugly for having dark skin and a wide nose. I was also shoved around and received threats to get cut, but I did nothing. I was scared. My self-esteem was very low, and I felt worthless. I laid low to avoid drawing attention, but that never helped.

Shauntanika was the meanest bully at my school. She made my three years of middle school a living hell. My grades were awful, and some of my teachers even considered me a slow learner. That lowered my academic confidence even further.

I once cut school with my friend Mary. My mom found out because we left our backpacks at home. I got the life beaten out of me, but it was worth not getting bullied for one day. The following week, another friend was standing outside of school waiting for someone. I spoke to her for a moment and started walking away. Then I heard someone scream, "Fight!"

I didn't want to watch, but I turned around, and there was a crowd of people in a circle yelling and fighting. I was so thrilled that I wasn't involved, but my happiness faded as soon as I saw the friend I just spoke to getting jumped.

Before the staff and police could stop the onslaught, someone sliced her face with a razor or knife several times. I couldn't believe it and instantly felt sorry for her. They took her away in an ambulance, and I never saw her again. This was one of the worst middle schools in the district. I feared for my safety every day and kept my head down to avoid drawing attention to myself.

I tried to get my brother to help, but he was too cool to deal with my issues. Complaining to my mother didn't help either. The boys were the worst sometimes. They would call me an ugly black bitch, pull my hair, and kick me in the hallway.

After a bully pulled my hair one day, I tried getting Jheri Curls again, but I got the same result, and my hair fell out. I could have just died. I knew nothing about suicide, but if I did, I would have ended my life.

I figured that when high school came around, things were going to get better. Unfortunately, things got worse. The bullying continued, and I no longer attended church.

Chapter 4 There Is An Order

After my dad left, my mom allowed my brother and I to listen to hip hop music. I first heard of the popular and militant hip hop group Tribe in 1990. They had a hit single out, and their music and style differed from other groups.

I was now 14 and looking for something to belong to. Their Black Boots Movement seemed ideal. Having no real friends or close family members, I figured, why not see how it goes? I asked my mom if I could go, and she said yes.

On my first day, I went to State Street, where their first office was located. I was nervous and didn't know what to expect. Would I fit in? Would they like me? These questions filled my brain. When I walked in, a sister named Pat instantly greeted me. She was the secretary and told me I could join the Black Boots Movement.

All I knew was that they were pro-black and "conscious." Being conscious meant you were in tune with the struggle of black people and were proud of your blackness. A conscious person was not seeking acceptance and assimilation. I wanted to learn more about my history and also desired love, so I went by their office every day after school for about two weeks.

One day I walked in, and all the members of Tribe were there. I was so excited that I could have jumped out of my skin. I played it cool and just smiled. That day, Pat explained to me that there was an order. Lord Master was the Overseer, and Prince was the Underseer. We had to greet these brothers with a special handshake and bend down like we were subordinates, and they were kings. So the day I met them, I was ready for the handshake when Lord Master asked, "Why do you want to join the family?" I responded, "I want to help black people." He and Prince smiled at me, then he said, "There are levels to it. You have to learn order and work hard. Then you can earn your crown."

Tribe wore red, black, and green leather crowns with an ankh in the middle. Some sisters and brothers had already earned their crowns. At first, I was afraid of Lord Master. He seemed a little intimidating, especially when he spoke. He always spoke in code and carried an enormous stick like in the music videos. Both he and Prince had their nostrils pierced. Prince seemed more relatable. I told myself I would earn a crown someday.

One evening, a member of the organization called my house to tell me about a mandatory meeting. I dropped everything and rushed over there as fast as I could. We were all in a circle. There were over thirty of us, and Lord Master said that we were on high alert with the Feds. I had no idea what that meant, but it seemed serious. We were preparing for a march over the Brooklyn Bridge the next day to protest our people's injustice.

That same night I met Willie Lockton. We called him the Headmaster. I knew about him from seeing him on the news, and there was even a movie made about him. He was a political activist and very intimidating. My first impression of him was a loud and angry man. He was yelling at the brothers and sisters there. I was told to greet him, and I did. He rudely asked, "Who's this?" I responded, "My name is Patrice. I'm new." Then he replied, "Ok." He then continued his conversation, which centered on hate for the white man.

His favorite word was "cracker ass cracker." I quickly learned that white people were our enemies. At least, at that time, that's what I thought. I learned that it was not ok to trust them, and not one white person had any good intentions. I was told that I needed to wear all black with combat boots, so I went home that evening and asked my mom if she could buy me some. I didn't think she would, but she gave me $80 to buy the boots. The following day I purchased some Doc Martens. I had my clothes and finally my boots. I was ready to go. Now I could fit in with everyone else. I was excited that I was finally a part of something bigger than myself.

That evening I got dressed and met them at the office, and we made our way marching in the streets with hundreds of youth and adults yelling, "No justice! No peace!" Police were everywhere. I had seen nothing like it. Once we began marching over the bridge, the police tried pushing the crowd back. I heard the crowd saying, "Fuck the police!" Things could have quickly gotten out of hand. Thankfully, the elders got on their loudspeakers and calmed everyone down.

We eventually made it across the bridge without too many incidents. The protesters threw bottles at the police. It was frightening, but I was with the Black Boots Movement, so the people protected us. They shielded us in a circle, and no one was breaking through, not even the police. I'm not sure what the protest accomplished, but Tribe, the Black Boots Movement, and Willie Lockton received a lot of love for spearheading the rally. I went home that night believing that all white people were bad, and they were the devil. They hated us and wanted to see us suffer and die, or at least that's what Willie drilled into my head.

I started going to the Black Boots Movement every single day, even on the weekends. I began meeting the other members. A man named Sensei was one member of the organization who stood out to me. He was weird, barely spoke, and always wore some kind of karate uniform. Sensei carried a stick and performed karate moves in Tribe's music videos.

Denise was a high-ranking member that wore a red, black, and green crown. I didn't care for her. She was mean and very condescending when she spoke to me. She carried herself as if she was prettier and better than everyone else. Denise was madly in love with Prince and there appeared to be competition between the female members for his attention. Pat was responsible for running the office and did whatever she was told. Her primary focus seemed to be recruiting members.

Rapper XY was a member. He was very mild-mannered, and I liked him as a person. He was always very kind to me.

Antoine was Lord Master's cousin. He seemed cool. My mom realized how much I enjoyed this group. One day she came to see the people that her daughter was hanging out with. We arranged a meeting at the office for her to meet the Lord Master and Prince. Her boyfriend accompanied her.

It was a very tense meeting. My mom maintained a very stern face as she sat across from them. After five minutes, she told me to go sit in the car. Several moments later, Prince popped up at the car window and assured me with a look that everything was ok. On the way home, my mom said she didn't like them and that they smelled funny, but she never said I couldn't go back.

Chapter 5 Get Out

Pat called me the next day about a mandatory meeting. By the time she called, the meeting was about to start. My mother and brother weren't home, so I had to take my little sister with me. She waited for me downstairs at the office.

When I arrived almost thirty minutes after it started, everyone was in a circle. I upset the Lord Master with my late arrival. He smacked me across my face so hard that my gold earrings flew across the room. I was in shock. One tear fell from my cheek.

While my face was ringing, he told me to drop and give him 20 push-ups. I never did a push-up before that moment, but I got down and tried. I tried my hardest for a minute, and then the Master told me to get up.

He explained that my tardiness was unacceptable and that everything had an order. Pat had this smirk on her face. I was at a loss for words, but the meeting continued. I only heard bits and pieces of him saying something about the Korean stores and a riot.

At the end of the meeting, Lord Master made it seem like it was my fault, but he had faith that I would do better. Then he greeted me with the special handshake, and I bowed down to him. The other members reassured me it was normal and not to worry about it. I went home that night, hurting and embarrassed. My dad previously did the same things to me as the Master, so I went back the next day as if nothing happened.

The following day was freezing cold, so I dressed extra warm. NYC cold is a special weather that makes your bones chill. I got in Willie Lockton's brown station wagon, and that day I met his granddaughter. She was about the same age as me, and we rode to Flatbush Avenue because this Korean store violated a black woman. Word spread that they assaulted her, and it caused a huge ruckus in the community.

Willie organized a protest outside of their place of business to run them out of the neighborhood. When Willie would yell, "Whose streets?" We would scream, "Our Streets!" Then he shouted that there would be funerals and not protests. Shortly after, the crowd began throwing bottles at the store. The riots and protests went on for seven months.

Once everything ceased, they sold their business to another Korean family, and everything went back to normal.

One day after school, I asked my mom if I could get a beeper because my organization had a hard time contacting me. My mom responded, "Well, that's just too bad. Either they can call the house phone or just wait until they hear from you." I didn't want to get smacked again, so I stole $20 from underneath her mattress and purchased a beeper. What I didn't know was that you had to pay $10 a month for a certain number of beeps. I still bought it anyway.

I had it for about a week until it fell off my hip and into a drain as I crossed the street. I guess that's what I get for being a thief. Around this time, I attended a Co-Ed School and dealt with repetitive bullying. One day a girl almost pulled the hair out of my scalp, and I ran to my brother's class for help. The entire class laughed at me, and I could tell I embarrassed him, so I left.

I was heartbroken and felt alone. I hated school. Not only was I failing the 9th grade, but I also had no one to talk to. I started cutting classes periodically and took the train to the Black Boots office. They were transitioning to a new building on Ashland place, so I skipped school to help Pat pack. One day she asked, "Why are you cutting class?" I told her I didn't like the school, and she just said, don't get in trouble.

When we finally moved to the new office, my mom found out about me skipping school. She was beyond pissed and kicked me out of her house. I couldn't believe I got kicked out for cutting school because I was an obedient child, aside from that. I was just deprived of some much-needed attention, but instead, I got put out.

I was 14 at the time and didn't know how to care for myself. Going to the Black Boots office in Brooklyn served as my only option. Pat was there with a few other members, and I told her what happened. She nonchalantly told me, "Don't worry. I will talk to the Lord Master and see what he says."

Me cutting school was only a small portion of my mother's problems. The woman that my father left us for gave him HIV. My mom had to take medication to make sure she didn't have the virus. All of this was thrown on her while being a full-time student, employee, and mother. My big brother kept getting in trouble, so she sent him to Rhode

Island to live with our dad and his twin brother Morris. I was really alone now.

Pat told me that the Lord Master and the Underseer Prince said that I could live in the office. I was kind of happy that they said yes, but I wanted to be home. Their office was better than living on the street, so I brought my bag upstairs.

Chapter 6 Seven

Shortly after the sunset that night, some brothers who reeked of smoke came up to the office. They pressured me to smoke, but initially, I resisted. The persistence carried on to where it felt like I didn't have another option. I didn't know exactly what they wanted me to smoke, but they said it was from the earth and would help ease my mind. I felt nothing at first, but then started feeling different, sleepy, and really high.

Shortly after their jokes, the Underseer came to the office and told me to take a pull of the libations, and I did. I sat back on the couch, and they were like, "Yeah sis!" So I guess I thought I was officially part of the family. Things started off fine. Tribe would be out of town all week for performances, and the office became my new home. I went to school occasionally. One day in front of the school, the principal, Mr. Mickens, approached me and asked, "Why are you messing with those people?" He began telling me how bad Tribe was, then Willie Lockton magically appeared. Willie periodically picked me up from school when he was coming from downtown Brooklyn. This week Tribe left town for performances, so I guess it was Willie's turn to make sure I was taken care of.

I had now been living with them for several months. I couldn't take a shower because there was only a tiny sink and a malfunctioning toilet. I went to school almost two hours early to sneak and take a shower. Sometimes I wondered why the members of the organization never invited me to their house to bathe. I was the informal secretary of their production company. I answered phones, took messages, gathered performance information, and made calls to the members for meetings.

One Saturday afternoon, while Tribe was out of town, Pat visited the office and told me to get ready because the Master Overseer wanted to see us. I complied and got dressed. Usually, we caught the train to meetings, but this time we caught a cab. I figured it must have been an important gathering.

The cab dropped us off in front of an illustrious hotel in Manhattan. On the elevator ride, which was all glass, I could see the entire hotel. Once we got to our floor, we walked to a suite, and she knocked on the door. The Master Overseer and seven other men from the Black Boots Movement were there. I greeted Master and DJ Hotep. Everything seemed normal. After a few minutes, Pat suddenly left the room without saying much. Before she could close the door, the Master told me to come by the couch. Then he said, "Sister, I want you to take down your jumper."

I had on a purple-striped short jumper from the clothing line, Cross Colors. Cross Colors was the main attire that Tribe wore as if they were sponsored by them. These grown men surrounded me, and I felt shaken, but I complied and took down my jumper. I didn't have any underwear on because I went without a shower again and couldn't wash my clothes.

After he took my jumper off, he told me to get on my knees, and then the Master began raping me in my rectum. I immediately went numb. All I could hear and see were the brothers saying, "Oh shit!" as if it turned them on. I don't remember how long he spent raping me, but once he was done, the rest of them took their turn on me. Seven men that I trusted. Seven men that were supposed to be my brothers. Seven men that I thought were supposed to protect me. Each one betrayed me to the darkest degree.

For a long time, it was dark outside when I looked up. Even if it was the middle of a sunny day. That event went beyond each molestation and sexual abuse experience. I was in complete shock.

After they had their way with me and fixed their pants, the Master told me I could get up and go clean myself off. I couldn't even look at myself in the mirror. I was beyond ashamed, and a million things were going on in my head. The more I wiped, the more blood I saw. I kept wiping until it was completely gone. I just stood there looking down. No tears, no emotions, nothing. I hooked up my jumper and made my way to the door.

Master said he was proud of me and that I had done really well. He gave his cousin Antoine, from North or South Carolina, some cash and said that I earned myself a really good meal. Master told him to take me back to the office and make sure I had something to eat. I wondered what happened to Pat, and why she left me? Antoine and I took the D train, and he acted as if nothing happened. Once we got closer to the office, he took me to Applebee's. I ate my entire meal, although I didn't have an appetite. After our meal, we went back to the office, and I got my pile of blankets to get ready to lie down. Once I laid down, Antoine climbed on top of me and penetrated me without my permission. Not only did I just get anally raped by seven men, Antoine decided that it was ok to break my virginity. I was only 14 years old and damaged. After that day, I was never the same.

Chapter 7 Weedie, Stop

Several days later, Underseer Prince popped up at the office with some chicken and fries. I ate like it was my last meal because I had starved for days. The day before he came, I found an old can of cat food and took it to the corner store to get a refund. I used the dollar to purchase a Debbie Cake, a quarter water, and one loose cigarette. The unfortunate events led me to do things I never planned on doing, such as smoking to help cope with reality.

Once I finished eating, the Underseer told me to come into the tiny restroom with him. Before I could close the door, he pulled down my pants and put me on the tin sink. The Underseer pulled his pants down and began forcing himself inside of me. He was six feet tall with a muscular frame, and I was barely taller than five feet and weighed 100 lbs. He was sweating, and it was hurting. I moaned from the pain as he kept forcing it until he was able to go inside me. After he finished violating me again, he threatened me not to tell anyone.

Thirty minutes later, the members arrived at the office for a meeting. Shortly after, we went to protest at an African burial ground in Manhattan. We protested for weeks back and forth, and finally, they gave up a portion of the area to commemorate the slaves. It served as a major victory. Black Boots, Willie Lockton, and Tribe received praise for their efforts.

A random guy showed up to the office a week later and told me that the Master Overseer wanted to see him. After I led him to the Master's office, I gave the guest an application to join the Black Boots Movement. Michael was his name, and he stood about six foot three and had red hair and a red mustache. He seemed a tad bit weird and traveled from Detroit to join the movement. He had a duffle bag draped across his shoulder, and I assumed he was going to stay with one of the members or at a hotel. The Master, Underseer, and some brothers brought Michael downstairs. After the Master returned upstairs, he told me that the new member would stay in the office with me.

I felt an extreme sense of discomfort, but I knew there would be repercussions if I spoke up. I was now living in a room smaller than a studio apartment with two grown men at the tender age of 14. Antoine and Michael were now my roommates. Neither had money to feed themselves, even though they served as the Master Overseer and Underseer's security. At the beginning of our tenure living together, they spent most of their time with Tribe. Pat occasionally came by to check in on me, but her time was dedicated to Tribe.

I never had enough to eat and was hungry all the time. It had now been over several months of isolation from my family. I reached out to my mom, but she still wanted nothing to do with me. I had no choice but to become a survivor. Every now and then, when I could sneak out, I'd pass by my mother's place, but she was never there. My baby sister was always home, so she would sneak me in, and I would eat as much as I could and then leave. My system worked for a while until the landlord snitched to my mom. It was a brownstone building, and my mom and sister lived on the top floor. Ms. Stevens was always nosey. My sister got grounded, and that was the end of the opportunity to eat regularly.

Things began getting worse by the day. I was no longer attending school because I was dirty and had no way to wash my clothes. Plus, I was sick of the bullying. Once summer came around, I was emotionally and mentally drained. Out of desperation, I contacted my Aunt Kim and told her I needed money for food. I met her in the Village at some restaurant, and she gave me $50.

I figured, okay, this is my time. I tried to tell her what was going on, and she laughed at me. "Weedie, stop," she said chuckling. I felt weird telling her, so I laughed along out of nervousness but said, "I'm serious, Aunty." It was just a big joke. I was already labeled as the bad kid because I was not home. Telling her was a big mistake, so I went back to the office. That night the Master came over and forced me to have sex with him. Then he patted me on the head and gave me $20. I was so hungry when I got up the next morning that I dashed to the corner store to get a hero and a 50 cent soda. I ate everything in record time, and my stomach immediately went to shambles.

Later that night, Michael broke my sleep by climbing on top of me to force my legs open and penetrate me. He was sweating profusely and penetrated me for what seemed like forever. Eventually, he got off me and laid on the couch while I was in a ball on the floor. Then he threatened me not to tell anyone, but I did. I told Pat. She took me to Brooklyn Hospital to get checked. I wondered why no one ever took me there after Lord Master, Prince, and the others raped me.

Shortly after we got settled in a doctor's room, Pat stepped out to make a call. After she came back in, she said we have to leave.

When we returned to the office, everyone was in a circle surrounding Michael. They asked me did he have sex with me. I quickly responded, yes. The Master became infuriated, then barked, "You didn't get permission, and there is an order!"

Michael received one of the worst beat downs I ever saw. He received repetitive punching and stomping. Every time he would drop, they would tell him to stand up, and punches would fly from every angle. I was in shock all over again. He was beaten so severely that his eye was bashed in. After the brothers were tired of beating him, they dragged him to a car, and that was the last I ever saw of him. Antoine and I remained behind after everyone left. He said if anyone asks you about this, tell them I never touched you.

The following day the rapper XY showed up at the office. The Master asked him to take care of me while they were out of town. I rarely saw him, but when I did, he was always very kind to me. Hanging with him gave me a break from the madness. I packed my two outfits in a plastic bag, and then he took me to his apartment, which wasn't far away in downtown Brooklyn. During my first visit to his house, I met his wife. She was a charming woman that appeared successful professionally and personally. She and XY mostly ate vegetarian food, and she held a high-level position with a sneaker company.

During my first night there, I remained awake until the sun came up. I was petrified of getting raped in the middle of the night. It was tough to fight my sleep on their couch because it was much more comfortable than sleeping at the office. Fortunately, that never happened. XY treated me like I was his little sister, and I hung out with him often.

That was the first time in a long time that I felt safe with a black man. It seemed like I was there forever, which was great for me, but it didn't last forever. Just as I was getting comfortable, I had to go right back to the office. My world was shattered, and I missed them as soon as I left. I began seeing less of XY because his music was doing very well, and it kept him busy.

Chapter 8 You Must Be Kidding

Soon I was back to my same routine. Pat took me to the Underseer's house on East 25th Street. Prince lived on that street in his mother's basement. I walked in, and the entire room was filled with comics and posters of the X-Men. I mean everywhere. His mom came downstairs briefly and said hello, then she left. Pat also left to go to the chicken spot. I desperately needed food, so I instantly became happy.

Moments later, that happiness was snatched from me when the Underseer forced me to have sex with him. This was becoming a regular thing now, and unfortunately, I wasn't surprised by any of it. Once Pat returned, we ate chicken and fries and carried on like nothing happened, even though Pat had to have known what had just taken place.

That day I found out that the Underseer had a daughter by one of the female members of the group. His daughter was roughly four years old. After I was over there for two hours, she came downstairs to give her dad hugs. He quickly rushed her back upstairs seconds after she entered the room.

Shortly after my 15th birthday, Tribe was in the studio working on their album. They sent for Pat and me to come to the studio. When we arrived, the Master held a pack of matches as he stood in the center of the studio. Once we walked in, he scooped something white in it and sniffed it. Next, the Master Overseer poured me a glass of liquor. The Underseer said they were pouring libations. Then someone passed it to me and told me to drink it. As soon as I tilted the cup, it burnt my lips and tongue. I tried to get out of it, but he told me to hold my nose and drink it. I started taking tiny sips, and the Master got upset, so I took one big gulp and started coughing. As soon as the drink hit my system, I became dizzy, and everyone started laughing. Once the laughs ceased, the Underseer went into the booth to record. The Master continued snorting cocaine, and he forced me to try it.

My defenses were down because of whatever they made me drink, so I inhaled it and felt a rush to my brain. Being forced to have sex with the Master was the last of my conscious memories of that night. Once it was time to leave, my period came down. Instead of them getting me clothes and pads, they made me get on the train with Pat. When we made it back to the office, they made me use tissues instead of pads. The insult to injury that night was returning home to the office during a blisteringly cold winter with no heat. One member brought me a thin ass wool blanket that was as thick as a sheet of construction paper.

Two days later, we had a late-night meeting, and they bought a huge bucket of KFC. That would be my first meal in over 48 hours. No one even checked on me after I was raped in front of everyone again. I called my mom earlier that day to talk, but she was on her way to Kings Plaza shopping mall. I wanted to finally tell her what was going on and that I wanted to come back home, but she shut me down and hung up in my face.

At the meeting, the Master informed us we were on high alert, and the FBI was watching us, so we had to walk light. The Original Recipe KFC held my undivided attention for most of the meeting, and I didn't retain much of what they said. It appeared he would never stop talking. Once he finished speaking, he and the Underseer got first dibs on the chicken. Next, the members with the crowns ate. By the time the bucket got around to me, there were only two measly wings and no sides. Everybody ate good except for me, but I had a plan to go in the garbage and eat what they discarded. I refused to starve that night. When they left, I tore through the trash and ate everything they threw away. Once I finished filling my stomach with their scraps, I wrapped myself in the wool blanket and went to sleep.

I starved consistently during that brutal winter. During one snowstorm, I couldn't take it anymore. I bound a rope around my legs to harm myself and get a trip to the hospital. I knew that would swell my legs up, and I was desperate to have a warm bed and some food. I called Pat, and she told me to go to Children's Hospital, and she would meet me there. I knew that if they admitted me, I would have a warm bed, shower, and some food. I was desperate. It overjoyed me when they kept me for the night. Pat acted as my guardian, so the hospital employees didn't ask many questions. I took tests, x-rays, and they injected me with some kind of iodine to see what was going on. I wasn't truthful with the doctors, and I told them I didn't know what happened. The doctor looked at me with a face filled with concern and asked, "Are you ok?" I looked at Pat as if I needed permission to answer, then whispered, "I just woke up like this."

My visit lasted for three days. I ate well for a change, watched cable television, and they even gave me a change of clothing. The nurses were kind to me and were sad to see me leave. They called Pat and told her I was being discharged and that she needed to pick me up.

I wasn't having that, so I quickly got dressed. I had a bad limp, so they gave me a cane. I figured that it was my best chance to escape. I walked to the train station. There were too many cops, so I couldn't hop the turnstile to get on the train. Black Boots hated cops, and I was trained to think all police officers hate black people. I ended up walking from downtown Brooklyn to my mom's house while it was heavily snowing.

My finger felt numb when I rang the doorbell. Shortly after I rang, my little sister opened the door. My mom reluctantly let me inside and made it clear that she had an attitude with me. I was thankful that she pushed her pride aside and gave me some baked chicken, rice, and veggies. After a few hours went by, I drummed up the courage to ask her if I could return home. My heart began beating like a boxing speed bag because I was so scared that she would say no. Once I asked, my mom looked at me deeply in the eyes and responded, "You must be kidding, right?" That was the end of the conversation. It broke my heart. I did not want to go back to the office. I was tired of being hungry and raped. All I wanted to do was consistently take a shower, brush my teeth, eat some good food, and sleep in a bed. Most of all, I wanted my mommy back, but I never asked again after that. After I wore out my welcome, I put my coat on, said my goodbyes, then walked back to the office.

Chapter 9 Don't Forget What I Said

I took my time walking because I knew they would torment me. When I arrived, the Master was there with a few other members. Shortly after I crossed the threshold, he asked, "Where were you?" I timidly responded, "I was walking around." As soon as I answered, he smacked me, then made me do push-ups. While I was on the ground, he barked at me that there is an order, and I will respect it. I thought that was the end until he made me get on my knees. While I was on the ground, he pressed a gun to the back of my head and told me that if I tried that shit again, he would put a bullet in my brain.

Those threats left me shook and influenced me for a long while. A couple of days later, Pat brought me to their video shoot that appeared to be at a crackhouse. They were rapping about how evil drugs were. I kept wondering why they would make a song like this when they were sniffing coke? However, I wouldn't dare ask that question. I was already in the doghouse, so I did my best to stay out of the way. When I arrived, the Master Overseer reached in his pocket and pulled out a bullet. He put it in my hand and whispered, "Don't forget what I said, sister." I bowed down and responded, "Yes, Master."

I didn't think it was possible, but the following days were worse. They were in the studio still recording, giving me coke, and having sex with me each time. I grew accustomed to the routine, and nothing surprised me. I became addicted to cocaine, and my body was craving it every day. The Master elevated his power over me by not letting me do cocaine without him. He began inviting me to his house in Crown Heights. He lived in a beautiful apartment complex with security at the front desk. One day Pat took me to his apartment, and it was pitch black inside except for a little lamp when we entered. We greeted him as always and sat on the floor by the living room table. Once I spotted coke on the table, my body instantly reacted because I wanted it. Pat took the first sniffs, then it was my turn. I felt better instantly and was able to drink a glass of vodka without feeling sick. While we were indulging, I thought the Master was by himself until the bedroom door opened.

To my surprise, a white woman walked out of the room. Coke was all over the table. She silently walked into the restroom, then walked back to the bedroom and acted like she didn't even see us. I thought to myself, "She's white, and they said white people are the devil." I remained there all night, getting high off coke and liquor, and didn't leave until

10:00 AM. Pat dropped me off at the office, high and hungry. It took forever to get sober, and I didn't fall asleep until three the next morning. The following day the Master gave me $10 to get something to eat, so I went and got a hero and two loose cigarettes. I couldn't finish my food because of the sharp pain in my stomach that felt worse than menstrual cramps. It finally stopped hurting once I cried myself to sleep that night.

Tribe began bringing me to local performances. Everybody dressed nicely in their Cross Colors, but I remained in the same clothes every day. My job was to wave the flag back and forth during the entire performance. My arms would get so tired that I would be ready to cry. One night we performed at the Billie Holiday Theater, and the flag got a little low. That pissed the Master off. When we got back to the office, he forced me to do push-ups. My arms felt like they already gave out before I started, but they didn't care and continued talking without acknowledging me.

All the other male and female members also did push-ups when they disobeyed a direct order. I know it embarrassed some male members. Here they are in their 30s, and they are letting another grown man smack them, punch them, or make them do push-ups. I was the youngest, so I felt like I was getting it the worst. I lived there and had no family support, so it was easy to get away with abusing me consistently.

Things got a little better when a guy named Seth joined the movement. He was so cool and funny as hell. Seth always made me laugh. I loved it when he came around. He was one of the nicest people next to XY and never tried anything with me. We were close in age, and when he had money, he made sure I ate. Seth even took me to his mom's house to eat. It was like having a big brother around. I hated it when he had to leave because I knew that the abuse would pick back up as soon as he left.

Rape started happening daily. Then this guy Keith started joining in on the abuse. I will never forget his face. He was tall, skinny with a long head, and a major overbite and crowded teeth. It was as if he knew when everyone would leave. He treated me like a rag doll and would ram himself inside of me. It hurt so bad every time. Then he would give me $10 or $20 and threaten me with, "You better not say shit."

When we had meetings, it was like everybody had a secret about me. It got to where bathing and brushing my teeth were luxuries. One time I went a month without brushing my teeth. Pat began feeling bad for me and occasionally let me bathe at her house. I was an emotional wreck.

The group had so much control over me that they allowed me to go to my grandmother's house for Kwanzaa. They knew I was too terrified to say anything. Right before the holiday, the Master took me by his place to clean up to make everything appear ok.

The fear that they instilled in me was enough that I wouldn't dare say anything. I went to my grandmother's house, and my entire family on her side was there. I was so happy to see them, but I was still hurting on the inside. Having to pretend like everything was ok robbed me of my temporary happiness.

My mom kept the same negative energy when I saw her in the living room. After I left from by her, I went to the kitchen, and my grandmother walked up to me then discreetly put a $100 bill in my hand. Once I smiled for the first time in a while, she stated, "When I hit the numbers, I am going to give you some more." No one couldn't tell me I wasn't rich. I made plans to eat every day for a change and not tell anyone about the money.

The money made me happy, but my real reason for being in the kitchen was to get some of my grandmother's infamous crab, mussels, shrimp, and rice medley. It was my absolute favorite, and I had three servings. To avoid my mom, I stayed in my Uncle Kevin's room. He was my favorite uncle. He lived with my grandmother because he was shot in the head during my early childhood. The shooter thought he was someone else but didn't realize that until he paralyzed my uncle for life.

Everyone loved my Uncle Kevin, and he had a deep affinity for our family and basketball. He was never the same again after the unfortunate tragedy because they forced him to wear a helmet for a long time. He had a distinct limp and suffered from seizures. His condition drove him to become an alcoholic. He hung out on the corner every day and drank himself into convulsions periodically. Sometimes he would fall and hit his head outside when he had seizures. Everyone in the neighborhood knew my family, so they always looked out for Uncle Kevin. We hung out a lot when I was younger because we both loved Michael Jackson. I think we were his biggest fans. I would go by him sometimes just to watch videotapes of Michael Jackson all day. That's part of what made us so close, but things changed when he began drinking heavily.

My Aunt Judy lit seven candles for each day of Kwanzaa. There were seven days, and each day had a significance for family, love, and community. I hung out with my cousins for the rest of the night until 10:00 PM, when everyone started making their way back home. I said my goodbyes to everyone, including my mother, but she had an attitude with me again. The only thing I wanted in the world was to come home, have her accept me, and feel loved. However, that was not about to happen.

While I walked to the train station, I thought about how much I missed my family. Those loving thoughts got shattered when thunderous gunshots rang out on Flatbush East 45th Street. People were running, and I immediately went into survival mode and ducked under a car. The shooting seemed like it lasted forever. Once the noise ceased, I got back up and hurried to catch the train. When I returned to the office, the Master continued the abuse. My brief and rare moments of happiness disappeared because he forced me to get high and have sex with him again. Days and months passed, and I grew fed up with the entire situation. I reached out to Willie's goddaughter, who had left Black Boots a while ago. She told me about a shelter called Covenant House and how they could protect me.

I planned to run away, but the shooting and the Master's threat to put a bullet in my brain still traumatized me. That fear kept me grounded until one hot summer day in June. No one came to the office several days in a row, and I barely ate during that time. I reached out to Willie Lockton's goddaughter for the address to the Covenant House and took a leap of faith.

Chapter 10 Are We Clear?

Once I made it to the Covenant House, I met an employee at intake. I omitted the information about me being homeless and told them I just needed a place to stay. Unfortunately, they didn't have a bed that day. They gave me a MetroCard and a sack lunch and told me to call in a few days.

As soon as I stepped outside, I noticed a car that looked familiar. It was the brown station wagon that belonged to Willie Lockton. My heart almost jumped out of my chest. As I went the other way, Willie yelled out, "Sister!" I reluctantly turned around, and he told me, "Come here, I want to talk to you." My knees felt like they were buckling as I walked over to his vehicle. I greeted him and bowed after I made it by him, then he told me to get in the car. Once I complied, he said, "I know what's been going on. I know what my son and the other brothers did to you. The elders want to have a meeting, and we will have a court proceeding. Then we will decide what to do with them." I did not understand what he meant by that, but I thought ok, finally. He said we were going to the office. My heart felt ran over. I told him I didn't want to go back there. He eased my mind by telling me he was in charge and assuring me that no one else will touch me.

It was the longest drive from 40th Street in Manhattan to Ashland Place in Brooklyn. When we arrived, the Master, Underseer, and a couple of brothers were there. Willie said he had to step out and take a call. When he walked out of the room, they told me to get on my fucking knees then put a gun to the back of my head. This time they were pressing it extra hard and reminded me not to say shit. The Master said it's about loyalty, family, and order. Then he pulled me up by the arm. Willie walked back in shortly after the Master pulled me to my feet. He looked at me then said, "I have to handle something. Let's go." Although I felt it was a setup, I was excited that he took me with him. When I got in the car, he turned the ignition and asked, "Are we clear?" I quickly responded, "Yes, Headmaster."

Twenty minutes later, we arrived at a voter's registration campaign to meet some elders. After we wrapped up there, he took me to his house in Queens. His wife, April, must have been at work or something because it was just us. We went down to the basement, and he poured a drink from his bar. He asked me if I wanted one, and I declined. Then he sat across from me and said, "Look, I will keep you safe, and I will take care of you if you take care of me." Headmaster looked down at his pants and then unzipped them. I cried out, "No, I don't want to." It made me sick to my stomach that he knew what they did to me and still attempted to do the same thing. After I kept refusing, he took me back to the office, and the abuse continued. One day Seth came by the office to chill with me. I trusted him, so I told him I wanted to leave. He told me that Willie owned a building in Harlem that he never visited. Seth suggested that I go there until I could get myself together.

I got to the point where I would make it out or die trying. Seth took me to a brownstone on 139th Street in Harlem. A mattress and an almost empty room were waiting for me. He gave me some cash and told me to stay there. I quickly fell asleep on the mattress and was awakened by a squeaking noise. The first thing that I saw when I opened my eyes were two rats that were the size of cats. I backed up against the window, trying not to scream, but they terrified me. I just knew that they were going to bite me. They crept closer, and I thought I would pee in my pants, but then the front door opened, and they took off back into the wall.

I stayed up all night and went back to the Covenant House the next day to see if they had any beds. The Manager said, not yet, but if I had a drug problem, they would take me into the drug program in a week. I told her I did, and then she set up an appointment with a substance abuse counselor the following week. If I got accepted into the program, I would go upstate for a year to a place for adolescence called "Day Top in Rhinebeck." Seth kept his word and didn't snitch. He was the only person I could trust. I went to his house hoping he was there, and he was. We talked for a while, and I hugged him, then left for my new journey.

Chapter 11 Enchanting

I stayed at the brownstone for a couple more days, then went back to Covenant House. After the meeting with the counselor, I received acceptance into the program. There was a waiting period before I would be transported there. I became cool with a few kids there because they were relatable, but I still had to watch my back. I mostly looked for jobs during the morning time and hung out with the other kids, so I wasn't alone. Finally, the time came for me to leave. I was nervous and happy. They took us to an intake center in Queens to apply for Medicaid. Hours later, they took us in a van to Manhattan on 40th Street by Bryant Park.

The day seemed dedicated to legalities, but they fed us well. One thing that stood out about that day was the number of priests walking around and talking. On the break, we stepped outside to have a cigarette that they provided us with. During that time, I unconsciously went through withdrawal symptoms from cocaine. I was tired, anxious, depressed, and moody, but the cigarette helped. The counselor stepped outside and informed us it was time to go upstate.

It took us a few hours to get there. When we arrived, the beautiful grass trail enchanted me at the front of the premises that sat on several acres of land. When we got there, they had to check our bags, but I didn't have any because I only came with the clothes on my back.

They gave us antibacterial soap to use on our hair and body in case we had lice. I felt refreshed after taking a shower. The water was hot, and I instantly felt clean. I had a toothbrush and was so happy because it had been so long since I brushed my teeth. I stayed in there for a long while, and they didn't rush me or anything. They let me take my time. Once I came out, the female counselor showed me to my room.

It was simple and very nice. I was so happy to have a bed to sleep in, but I didn't show it. They gave me a fresh pair of underwear and clothes, which were some things I hadn't had in a very long time. After I dressed, the same counselor asked did I smoke cigarettes. I said yes, and she gave me two cartons of generic menthols. Surprised, I said, "Wow, thanks!" We then went to the cafeteria.

She told me to get settled, and she'd see me in a little while. There was a table with peanut butter, jelly, and 15 loaves of bread and some iced tea. There was also a microwave. Most of the kids there were Latino, black, and white. Every race you could think of was under one roof with the same problem, drug addiction. I sat at the table by myself, just looking around, checking out the scene, and feeling awkward.

Then a girl walked up and asked my name. I said, "Patrice." She said, "My name is Trish. What's your drug of choice?" I made a confused face, then answered, "Cocaine and weed." Once Trish told me she was in for the same thing, and from Brooklyn, I felt a connection. She introduced me to the other girls she chilled with and broke down the do's and don'ts. Although everyone in the circle opened up about their story, I made up a fairytale. I made it seem like I came from a wholesome home with two parents and siblings with no issues except a drug problem.

They called us for dinner, and we all walked to the cafeteria. We got our trays and cups and then got our food. We sat down together, and the food was great. They served us a chicken sandwich and rice with veggies. It was nice knowing that I would eat three meals a day plus a snack.

Everybody had something to say about how skinny I was. They wouldn't have cracked those jokes if they knew what I went through. I laughed the wise remarks off. Trish encouraged me by saying, "Girl, with the abundance of bread, peanut butter, and jelly around here, you will gain weight quickly." It made me feel better that she had my back.

Since I first arrived on a Friday after dinner, we made popcorn and tried watching a movie. The film was boring, so we opted to head outside to smoke and chill on the grass under a beautiful tree. The sky was so beautiful, and the stars looked like they were coming towards us. I had never seen anything like that before in my life.

When 10:00 PM rolled around, it was time to go to sleep, so we made our way back to the little cottages. It was co-ed, but they housed us in different buildings. My roommate was an Italian chick. After she introduced herself, we talked almost the entire night. She dominated most of the conversation and vented about how she was addicted to coke and her life story. Our commonalities made me comfortable, but the fear of a Tribe or Black Boots member showing up kept me from falling asleep.

I made sure not to call anyone to protect myself from being found. I couldn't take any risks. The first week was rough. Not because the place was awful, but because it was lovely there. It was a challenging change. We had daily group therapy sessions. The counselors were cool, and the unique part was that they were all ex-addicts. It was a blessing that they could relate to the addiction side of things. They assigned us chores such as cleaning our rooms and the facility, which didn't bother me at all.

I was still in fear for my life. I just knew they were going to find me. I didn't get comfortable for months. My sleeping patterns were off, but I was pushing through. I was four months clean. The group sessions were very supportive as far as my addiction was concerned. I wasn't craving like in the beginning, plus I was staying busy and actually having fun.

They would take a group of us into the city to have pizza and a soda. This was the best pizza I ever had. It had green olives in it, and I was in love. To top it off, we also had ice cream. I was so excited. My childhood was snatched from me. Therefore, these little pleasures I was now enjoying, including playing catch and basketball, were the best.

Although things were trending upward, I remained fearful. Sometimes at night, it felt like I was dying. My chest would hurt, and my heart would race. I didn't know it at the time, but these were panic attacks. After suffering one the very next morning, I put a smile on my face and acted like I was doing great.

Everyone received family visits except for me, and I felt like an outcast. I grew paranoid about what they thought about me. I reached out to the one person I knew would visit me, my Aunt Judy. I didn't give her too many details and only told her I was in a drug program. The following week she showed up for a visit. Once we locked eyes, she ran up to me and gave me the biggest hug and kiss. I was thankful that we had more than small talk. We went outside, and she filled me in on the family and her ambitions to get involved in the film industry. It was just nice to have someone there, showing me concern and love. Also, she twisted my hair and brought me a white hoodie. Previously, the only clothes I had were donated by staff and some residents. I was grateful, but it was nice to have something of my own. She was there for three hours, and then our visit was over. Before my Aunt Judy headed back to Brooklyn, she hugged me and told me she loved me.

Chapter 12 Marathon

After being there for a while, I built some trust with the crew, and Trish became my best friend. She was also a lesbian, and I knew I was too. Trish made me feel comfortable about my sexuality. Although I never had a girlfriend or wanted sexual intercourse with a woman, I knew who I was. One day our counselor walked up to my group and said that we were having a marathon.

We had to be in a locked room for 24 hours and tell all of our traumatic stories or issues. Everything spoken had to stay within the group. If anyone repeated anything, they would get kicked out of the program. It remained on my mind all day. I contemplated venting about the truth or fabricating a fairytale. I assumed that they wouldn't believe me, anyway.

After dinner, it was time. We were told to get our blankets and pillows and put our pajamas on. My group was six people and a female counselor. She started off by saying, "This is confidential. This is a place to leave all your pain and secrets. This is where you begin to heal." That made us comfortable, and one by one, everyone told their story. It shocked me that many people experienced similar situations as myself. We were not allowed to go to sleep. We stayed up until everyone told their story or truth.

When it was Trish's turn, my heart went out to her. She went through so much pain. I was next up behind her, and my heart began racing after they called my name. At first, I didn't know what to say or where to begin. The counselor broke the ice by telling me to start from anywhere. I took a few deep breaths then began telling some of my story, but I omitted the most gruesome parts. As I looked around while I vented, Trish, my counselor, and the other female residents were in tears. I felt slightly freed after venting about my journey, but not telling it all kept me from feeling liberated.

After twenty-four hours expired, someone knocked on the door. They served us a huge breakfast at the perfect timing. Releasing all that information was emotionally draining. The drain that night didn't compare to how drained I felt when Trish left the program the following year. She gave me her mother's number, and we promised to stay in touch.

I reverted to isolation for the next several weeks until I met a polish chick named Jennifer. We bonded instantly. My aunt Judy finally found out where my dad lived. I earned a day pass, and I used it to visit him. When I called him, he sounded happy to hear from me. Jennifer was my escort to the city. A counselor dropped us off in Manhattan. Jennifer went to see her friends, and I went to see my dad. I wasn't a snitch and understood that she missed her friends.

My dad seemed happy for a change. We spent the entire day talking, and then we went to KFC. Things seemed to come together for him. He offered me a place to stay after they released me from the program. I was so happy because I didn't know where I would go. After we finished, I reconnected with Jennifer. We both talked about our day and waited until the van picked us up for our trip back upstate. As soon as we got back, we had to take a drug test. I wasn't worried at all and passed. Unfortunately, several others failed the random drug test.

Chapter 13 Where Is Your Coat

A few months later, it was time for me to leave. While I met with the counselor to prepare for my discharge, they called my dad. He surprisingly held his word about offering me a place to stay. Several weeks later, I was back in New York living with my dad.

I kept my clothes in a big box until I could afford a dresser. I wanted to work right away because I wanted to get my own place. Thankfully, I found a job at the bodega in my neighborhood as a cashier. A week after working there, I received my first paycheck, and I stashed it under my pillow. I calculated that it would take five months of spending nothing to get my place.

Living with my dad started off fine. One night after several weeks of living together, he came home with bloodshot red eyes. When he began acting weird, I immediately thought he was smoking crack again. I asked him why he was looking at me crazy, then he sucked his teeth and went to the bathroom. Moments later, I began smelling something like burning rubber. It pissed me off, and I spent the rest of the night plotting on a way out.

I left the next morning without saying a word. When I got back home, there were a bunch of people there, and the house smelled funny. My dad called me by my childhood nickname and said, "Come here, Weedie." I ignored him and went to my bed.

Once I got to my room, I searched high and low for the $100 I hid but couldn't find it. When his company left, I approached my father about the missing money, and he asked did I check the room good. I responded, "Yes, but it's not there." Then I asked him if he took it. He instantly got defensive and said he would never steal from me. He even helped me look for it, but I knew in my heart that he stole it.

Later that night, my dad spent forever in the bathroom. I kept knocking on the door and telling him to hurry. Then I heard someone else in there with him, and they began whispering. Once I heard the whispers, I sat back on the bed. Less than a minute later, a lady strung out on crack exited the bathroom. My dad followed behind her, and so did a powerful odor. I was beyond pissed and asked him about why he lied to me about giving up crack.

He was so fucked up that he pulled out his penis and urinated all over the clothes I had in the box. After I pushed him and began crying out to him, he responded, "Oh shit. I'm sorry." Then he got upset with me like it was my fault and yelled, "If you don't like it, then you can get the fuck out, bitch!" Next, he grabbed me and tried to shove me through the wall. Once I fought him off, I ran out of the apartment. He chased me and yelled, "Weedie wait! I'm sorry!"

I frantically ran to the train station without a destination in mind. I couldn't stay with my aunt because she only had a studio apartment. Next, I went to my Uncle Kevin's place and told him what happened. He allowed me to stay, but he lived in a one-room apartment also and had a drinking problem.

I loved him dearly, but it only lasted for two days. Next, I went to my grandmother's house. She was still persistent that she would hit the lottery one day. When I asked her if I could stay, she said that when she hits the numbers, she will get me a room. Then she gave me $20, and I left. I hung out at the corner store by her house because I had nowhere else to go. Luckily, the guy who owned the corner store noticed me loitering and said that I could sleep in the store. At first, I declined, then he asked, "Well, what are you going to do? Stand here all night?" He let me in and closed the gate in the back of the store where there was a bed and a TV. He let me sleep there for a week, but I had no place to bathe. After my seven days were up, I began sleeping on the D train.

I never imagined my life resulting to this. During my upbringing, I saw homeless people on the train and wondered how they could sleep on the train like that. Well, that became me. It was rough the first couple of weeks. I was hungry and had no way to get money.

After a few weeks, some other homeless teens told me about a center in Times Square. The place was a savior. They provided meals, clothes, a place to wash clothes, and a MetroCard.

I began going there every day and tried to avoid looking homeless on the train. It became obvious when I started seeing the same people every morning when I would wake up. My pride stopped me from panhandling. Some nights became horrific. Creepy men began masturbating in front of me, and I grew afraid that someone would try to rape me.

One night I was exhausted and couldn't keep my eyes open. Shortly after I drifted off, a man pulled out his penis and told me he would give me money for oral sex. I immediately jumped up and got off at the next stop.

That incident played a significant factor in developing insomnia. I grew accustomed to getting an hour of sleep during the day when the train was packed with people going to work. I took different train routes to try avoiding perverts, but it didn't matter because they were everywhere. Crying became consistent, and sometimes people asked me if I was ok. Each time I would always clean my face up, then lie and say I'm ok.

One brutally cold January morning, I accidentally ended up by the ferry. I was shivering uncontrollably because I didn't have a coat on, as usual, that winter. I wanted people to think I was ok with no coat in the winter.

A white woman sitting on the bench across from me asked, "Where is your coat?" I shamefully responded, "I don't have one." She replied, "I will be back." To my surprise, she returned ten minutes later with a coat and hat for me. I smiled and thanked her, then she said, "You don't look like you do drugs." I assured her I didn't, and she reached in her pocket to give me $20. The act of kindness wasn't over. She provided me with a cup of hot chocolate and a doughnut.

For a moment, I didn't feel homeless. I rarely left the station that winter because of the bone-chilling weather. Later that evening, I journeyed off to find a bodega. I purchased a turkey and cheese sandwich with a 50 cent soda for $2, then vowed not to spend any more money.

The following day I went to get some food and clean clothes from the place that the homeless teens recommended. I was beyond grateful and hung out there all day. They even offered acupuncture for those of us that were stressed out. So I said what the hell and tried it. The acupuncturist stuck long needles into my face. I laid there with the lights out for an hour. When he came back, I was knocked out.

He later said it took a while to wake me up. When I opened my eyes, I forgot where I was and jumped up scared. The acupuncturist said, "Look at your space. Look around. You're okay. You're safe." I calmed down, and he removed the needles. He told the counselor what happened, and she suggested that I come once a week to therapy.

My attitude was that I did not need counseling. She said, "It is good to talk about the things we go through. It helps to heal." I had no idea what she was talking about. I didn't need to heal because I felt fine and wasn't with Tribe or Black Boots anymore. I already put them in the back of my head and tried to forget them.

One day the counselor told me about a job opening at a French bakery that I passed every day. I told the counselor I didn't have an address, and she said that I could use the center's address. She didn't stop there. She also gave me some slacks, a button-down shirt, and some dress shoes that barely fit.

I never had a real interview before, so my nerves were through the roof. The counselor gave me a mock interview to help me prepare. Her first question was, "Why do you want this job?" My answer was, "Because I need money." She laughed and said, "Of course, but you need to say something like, I'm a team player. I work well with others, or I enjoy working in the restaurant industry." She asked a couple more questions, and then I made my way to the bakery.

Each step on the way there hurt because my shoes were a size too small. When I crossed the threshold, I smiled then said, "Good morning. Are you hiring?" A lady named Mrs. Brown looked me up and down, then responded, "'Yes, hold on. I will grab you an application." Once I quickly finished with the form, she looked it over and asked, "Do you have time for an interview?" I answered yes, almost before she could finish her sentence.

Mrs. Brown told me to have a seat at one of the tables and that she would be back in a couple of minutes. I looked around at the other employees while I waited and tried to calm myself down. She reappeared fifteen minutes later, and she said, "Ok, Ms. Patrice. Let's begin." She asked a bunch of questions, and I answered them to the best of my ability. Every time she made direct eye contact with me, I kept putting my head down. I kept thinking the whole time she's not going to hire me. Once I lost faith that I would get the position, the phone rang, and she asked me to hold on.

After Mrs. Brown was done on the phone, she informed me that I got the position and asked when I could start. I responded, "Right away." She cracked a grin then said,

"How about next Monday morning at 7:30." I hid my sadness that it was six days away from my starting date.

As she walked me to the door, she continued, "Bring in your birth certificate, social security card, and an ID on your first day. You will also need a pair of black slacks and black shoes or sneakers. We will provide you with a uniform shirt."

I walked out sad because I didn't have any of those items or enough money to get them. When I returned to the center, I informed the counselor of the good and bad news. She told me not to worry about it because the program had connections to take care of everything. Then she said, "I'm so proud of you. We sent other teenagers there to get a job, and they would leave without one. I knew you were different." She handed me a MetroCard and sent me to four different offices to apply for my identification.

During the week leading up to my new job, I slept on the trains and daydreamed about having my own place soon. For some reason, I thought I would get a big fat check. I made all these big plans because of the new job that barely paid above minimum wage. I went to the center early Monday morning around 5:00 AM to prepare for my first day. The shift started with a quick tour.

Everything smelled so good, especially the freshly baked raspberry croissants and sandwiches. My mouth was watering so much. After the tour, my supervisor gave me a towel and a bottle of disinfectant spray to start by cleaning the tables.

I was so happy to clean the tables, and I did it with the utmost pride. The staff warmed up to me fairly quickly. Once my lunch break came, I inquired about a soup and sandwich combo, but it was $10 and out of my price range. The supervisor saw my reaction to the price and said that I could get something to eat since it was my first week. I ate well and had one of those raspberry croissants I smelled earlier.

The best part of the job was that we could take the leftover baked goods home. I did my best to pretend I wasn't starving outside of work. The first week went by great, and I received a $100 paycheck that I was able to cash at work. After payday, everyone planned to go to the bowling alley to chill and have some drinks. I didn't drink but still went. I had such a good time. It felt good to have some genuine friends and co-workers. Around midnight, reality sat in. Everyone was going back to their homes, and I didn't have one.

We went our separate ways because we all had to be at work early the next morning. I rode the D train all night until the drop center opened at 5:30 AM where I took a shower and got ready for work. Being homeless put a limitation on how great things could be. Bags became mainstays under my eyes. I laughed off my co-worker's jokes about my sleepiness and felt too embarrassed to tell them the truth.

A week after I felt I couldn't go on any longer, a counselor presented me the opportunity to stay at a faith-based shelter operated by nuns for a week. Most of the shelters took single moms, or they were just filled with crackheads, so I was hesitant at first, but eventually gave in.

The nuns at the shelter on the Lower East Side were expecting me and very welcoming. After they finished greeting me, they laid out the rules, which included no drugs, guns, and sex, then led me to my room. The dull room felt like a five-star hotel suite. It felt like I fell asleep before I closed my eyes that night. Thankfully, I didn't have work the next morning because I didn't wake until noon. I might have slept longer if a nun didn't knock to see if I was ok. After I assured her I was fine, she brought me breakfast. I got a record amount of sleep that day. Once I finished the meal, I went back to sleep until it was dinner time.

My tenure at the shelter lasted two weeks. The nun woke me up on a Saturday morning to inform me they had to make room for another woman, and it was my last night. I cried until I got dehydrated on my last night at the shelter.

Chapter 14 Paranoia

The following morning I gathered my stuff and was back on the streets again. As much as I thought that getting rest at the shelter helped, it backfired. I grew accustomed to sleeping in a typical setting, and I had a hard time readjusting to being homeless. My supervisor became fed up with my late arrivals. Before I knew it, I was on my third strike. I tried so hard to get to work on time, but was drained mentally, physically, and emotionally. I skated on thin ice for two months until they gave me the pink slip that July.

The depression sat in more profound than ever after someone handed me my last check. I immediately became glued to the train and my misery. I was too embarrassed to go back to the center. My hourly wage didn't pay me enough to save, so I was back to starving again in no time. Desperation sat in on Friday night while I watched a woman eat a sandwich. When we arrived at her stop, she sat her sandwich down and left without it. I guess she forgot, so I sat there and ate it. At this point, I didn't care who saw me. I was hungry, dirty, and smelly. I just knew somebody was going to find my body, and that would be the end of me. I was taking the same train every day, so people started noticing me and would feel bad.

They started giving me food and water all the time. I wasn't completely starving, but I really wanted my life to end.

When winter came around, the D train had no heat, so I switched to the C train. After I drifted off to sleep my first night on the new train, a nudge awakened me shortly after falling asleep. Once I opened my eyes and saw a police officer, I quickly said, "I am getting off the train." He responded, "It's ok." Then a white woman standing next to him asked if I was hungry. Once I acknowledged the thunderous pains in my stomach, the lady, who introduced herself as Grace, asked me to follow her when she got off at the next stop.

When we got off at West 4th Street, she began explaining to me that she worked for an organization called Pathways to Housing, which was on 23rd Street in Manhattan. They helped homeless people transition into apartments and assisted them with furniture and other resources. We walked to a diner and had a feast that included pancakes, eggs, grits, and the works. I was stuffed. She talked the whole time, and I barely heard a word she said.

She wanted to go to her office and cover the program rules and assign me a permanent social worker. Things felt too good to be true, but maybe changes were on the horizon. Our destination on 23rd Street was a tall and beautiful building. I felt embarrassed about my condition, but Grace didn't acknowledge it. After we got off the elevator, she led me to a large office with a bunch of smiling faces and welcoming people.

The Director was the first person she introduced me to. He shook my dirty hand as if it were clean and had a friendly smile. After they walked off and asked me to wait in the office lobby, a friendly black man approached me and said, "Hi Patrice, it's nice to meet you. I'm Winston Chapman, and I am going to be your social worker."

I didn't trust him one bit. My distrust had nothing to do with him. The past trauma from my father, the Black Boots Movement, and bullies made me lose trust in any black man during that time. I was very cold towards Mr. Chapman, although he was very patient and kind. I assumed his kindness was a plot to reel me in and take advantage of me. Once we wrapped up our initial meeting, he gave me an address to a place where I could stay until they found me an apartment.

My mind raced about what could go wrong, but just the thought of living alone made me excited. Mr. Winston sweetened the pot when he said that I would get a voucher and that we would go search for some apartments where the rent would be $30 a month. I couldn't imagine there being any more good news until he said that they would help me get furniture, food, and schooling.

The following morning I showed up at 10:00 AM to go apartment hunting with him. Before we left the office, he bought me breakfast and arranged a therapist appointment for me the following week. I had so much joy inside, but I refused to show Mr. Winston. He showed transparency by admitting that he didn't like any of the apartments we looked at throughout the day. However, both of us were fond of the last unit we viewed.

The last apartment was on Lefferts place in Brooklyn. I instantly loved the studio apartment on the first floor. It was a small brick building with only six apartment units. Everything was separated inside the apartment. The family-oriented neighborhood made it even more attractive. Kids were riding their bikes up and down the street. The older members of the community hung out on their stoops. My paranoia still lingered because I loved the enormous windows. I could be aware if anything were to jump off.

The organization held its end of the deal and made a far-fetched dream come true. After two long years of sleeping on the train, I finally had my own place. Along with a furnished home, they gave me a stipend to get clothes because I had nothing. Grace took me to Old Navy and a few other stores to stock my wardrobe. I didn't know what size I wore in anything. I felt so special that the program moved mountains for me and gave me a sense of normalcy.

Once they settled me into the apartment, Mr. Winston gave me $100 worth of gift certificates for the supermarket, two weeks' worth of train tokens, and warm congratulations. After he left, I walked around the place ten times, then went outside to stand in front of my building to let it all sink in. Something as simple as a hot shower felt like a luxury. It had been two years since I took a shower in a clean restroom without having to wear slippers to be fearful of catching something.

Reality sat in when I woke up the following morning. I could no longer convince myself that I was living a dream. After I went to the store to grab some groceries, I pigged out and watched television for the rest of the day. I had gone so long without watching TV that I overly enjoyed the commercials. "Martin" became my favorite show after one episode. I wished I could have binge-watched it until it was time to return to the office.

I prolonged seeing the therapist until Mr. Winston told me it was mandatory on my next office visit. After I completed that step, they offered to help me find employment. The idle time and desire to work made me take advantage of the next available therapist appointment.

The therapist was a shy white man with glasses named Dr. Savage. Thankfully, his personality did not match up with his name. He asked me a lot of questions about my life and family. My life was moving so fast that I felt like I was catching up with everything while I vented to him. I told him my father died because he was dead to me. My brother got arrested for murder at 17, and I didn't believe he did it. My sister lived at home with my mom. I hadn't called her in a few years because of how she left me in the streets to be preyed upon. The session flew by, and Dr. Savage suggested that I see him twice a week.

The program gradually improved my trust for others. I left the therapy session not knowing how to feel, but my mind was eased once I got the news that I'd be starting a new position. My job duties included filing paperwork, making copies, answering phones, and occasionally helping residents at apartment buildings. Some people I worked with had major mental illnesses, and they frustrated me sometimes with their mood swings, but I did my job.

After a few sessions with Dr. Savage, I became comfortable. He suggested that I contact my mom to see how it goes. It scared me to call her, but I assumed that she would show me some love for a change because I was doing better. I desired her love and attention for years, and I was willing to do anything for it. My anxiety caused me to put it off for the next few days.

Once I finally gained enough strength to call her, it felt like my heart would beat through my chest. When she picked up the phone, I spoke before she could say hello. After I greeted her, she asked, "Weedie, how are you?" I wasted no time catching up and told her all about my good news. While I poured out my heart and sought affirmation and happiness, my mom acted as if she were talking to an unwanted acquaintance. Once I saw that I couldn't get through to her, I invited her to therapy so that we could work on our relationship. To my surprise, she agreed to come the following week.

My mom's ice-cold demeanor accompanied her to Dr. Savage's office for our therapy session. I almost forgot what a hug felt like, and she declined to give me one. The doctor started off the session by letting her know that I had a rough few years and suggested that we remain in touch from now on. My mom's response was, "Hmm, hm." When it was evident that she had nothing else to say, Dr. Savage turned to me and said, "Patrice, you can start."

I took a deep breath and said, "Mommy, I went through a lot with Tribe and Black Boots." She cut me off and interjected, "Like what?" with an attitude. I continued and began telling her about the story at the hotel. Then she abruptly cut me off to say that she couldn't hear this right now. Before I could respond, she stormed out of the session. Dr. Savage and I were unsuccessful at trying to get her to come back. While I cried with my head on the desk, he told me not to take it personally because it was a lot of information for her to handle at once. Dr. Savage pleaded for me to give it some time before I left his office.

The incident with my mom influenced me to stop going to therapy. I didn't see the light at the end of the tunnel with our situation. The fallout didn't prevent me from being consistent with my work and newfound happiness, but nightmares began altering things. I kept seeing the Master Overseer and the Underseer in my dreams. It was always the same dream of them attacking me and putting a gun to my head. I would fight back, but it wasn't enough because they could hold me down. Paranoia crept into my nights, and I began feeling like someone was watching me.

I didn't tell anybody about it for a long time because I didn't want anybody to think I was crazy. Plus, the black community always shunned mental health problems. I figured I could deal with it on my own. By this time, I had a decent relationship with Mr. Winston, and he treated me like I was one of his daughters. He tried nothing with me, and it was shocking because that's what I was used to.

Having consistency with my baby sister made everything better. Although I didn't successfully reconnect with my mom, I reconnected with my youngest sibling, Fallyn. She slept over periodically and made the nightmares better by joking about my chaotic sleeping habits. I laughed it off because I couldn't open up to her about my life story.

Fallyn asked many questions about the way I carried myself. It was then when I realized that I related my behavior to PTSD. My mental health began scaring me when I desperately avoided sleep because I was afraid to have nightmares. Energy drinks, no water, and minimal sleep kept me in a vegetative state throughout most days. I was moody and quick-tempered, especially with black men that made advances toward me. If they made a comment like, "What's good, shorty?" I would lash out. This carried on for months.

I was on the verge of forgetting that my father existed until Fallyn told me she spoke to him. I didn't react to the news until she told me she gave him my address. That infuriated me, but I couldn't be mad at her. I directed all of my anger towards him and what I was going through. A few days after receiving the news, he showed up to my doorstep at the break of dawn. The first thing I noticed was the sores on his face.

Early into our conversation, he began pleading for help until his social security and disability check came in and a place to stay. I don't know what soft spot he provoked in my heart, but I gave him a place to lay his head. I also let him use my phone to call his social worker. He gave her my address and assured me he only needed to stay with me for two weeks tops.

I fed him and treated him how he should have treated me. During dinner on his third night, he apologized for the past, but I didn't accept it. On the morning my father's check came, he told me he'd give me $300 after he cashed the check. While I watched him walk down the street, I wondered how many years would go by until I saw my father again. His actions reduced me back to reality. His stay drained my pockets and food supply, and I am still waiting on that $300.

Chapter 15 My Best Option

After going a few days with an empty stomach, I went back to the Pathways for Housing for some gift certificates. Unfortunately, Mr. Winston was out in the field when I stopped by. The only social worker available questioned me about why I was out of food so fast. I told her about my dad's health condition and the gist of what happened. She sympathized and gave me $75 worth of gift certificates, so I could get some food and free movie passes.

I hadn't been to a movie theater since I was a kid. I didn't even know how to have fun and be good to myself. It was like I had some sort of delay like I was an adult with the mind of a 14-year-old. It was weird. I had to learn things that should have already been taught to me. I had never been to a club with friends. I had never been on a date with a girl yet, although I knew I liked girls. I never had a girl's night out. I felt like some weirdo freak. I hated myself. I thought I was ugly and unworthy of love.

One day on the train back from Manhattan, I ran into my first friend at the program upstate, Trish. She stated that she had been looking for me. I felt comfortable opening up to her about being homeless and inviting her to my new place. We quickly made up for the lost time, and she invited me to hang out with her in the Bronx the following weekend.

The next week flew by as I hoped it did. I met Trish's family before we stepped out. Her spouse was gracious, and they were raising her kids together. They were adorable children. I couldn't say the same about the environment. The Bronx was one of the toughest neighborhoods in New York. Trish seemed to know everyone in the community. She tried hooking me up with several women, but none garnered my interest. I still had a great day. Later that night, she took me to my first gay club. There were so many people packed into one place that my heart raced every moment.

I baby-sat my drinks at the bar, while Trish danced the night away. That worked in my favor because I had time to mingle with the bartender. Once the DJ announced the last call, she gave me her number and told me I better reach out. I threw her number away with my last drink, and Trish and I caught the train back home.

The club wasn't my thing, but I enjoyed every moment. Trish and I began hanging out every other weekend, but we enjoyed two different lifestyles. The social interactions paid off subconsciously. For a while, my nightmares subsided, and I was sleeping for about six hours a night.

Shortly after I stopped linking up with Trish, my nightmares began reoccurring. I felt worthless all over again. The mental storm caused a snowball effect, and I began neglecting my responsibilities, such as my rent, health, and job. I convinced myself that taking medicine would help, so I started taking sleep aids. Death seemed like my best option. The pills didn't seem to work until I woke up one morning in Woodhull Hospital. Shocks from my stomach getting pumped awakened me.

Shortly after I arrived, they asked for my next of kin. At first, I said no, but they told me I couldn't be released without having someone pick me up. I gave the doctor my mother's number, although I didn't think she would appear. If she did, I knew she would arrive with an attitude. Once reality set back in, I became angry that I was still alive.

My mom showed up in the emergency room two hours after they called her. Before she offered me a hello, she asked, "Why would you do this?" I responded with tears. The tears came out at a faster rate once I got the news that I had to go to a psych-ward.

I woke up feeling frail on my first morning at the psych-ward. A nurse came in shortly after I opened my eyes to check on my well-being and vitals. My below average weight worried the nurse, and she insisted that I ate a meal. I resisted, but the nurse motivated me to consume something once she told me I needed to eat if I planned on going home anytime soon.

Once the nurse finished, she brought me down the hall to see a psychiatrist. His warm personality made me feel a tad bit comfortable. After we got past small talk, he asked, "Did you want to kill yourself?" When I responded yes, he did his best to restore hope in my life. After we wrapped up, he prescribed medicine for my depression.

I refused to take it for the first three days. Once my first few days went by, I met some people at the psych-ward who also tried to end their lives. They all faced different issues but seemed ok. I figured that if I took the medicine, I could get out of there and succeed at killing myself. I became cool with some patients, but I kept my distance and gave them a fake backstory.

My mom and Aunt Judy visited me occasionally. My mother's increased concern intrigued me. It wasn't enough to right her wrongs, but it lifted my spirits. The medicine was working, although I felt periodic tremors. The doctor assured me that the side effects would go away in a few weeks.

One nurse took a special liking to me. During a night shortly after the side effects from the medicine kicked in, she crept into my room and asked if I was gay. I paused for a second, then responded yes. The nurse started flirting with me and said she wanted to see me outside of the facility. It caught me off guard because she was an employee there, and she had a husband. I despised cheaters because of what one did to my mom. Her approach was distasteful because there I was, going through so much, and she is trying to hit on me. I played along while she made her advances but thought very little of her.

Thankfully, one week later, my doctor said I could leave in a few days. It was bittersweet because I felt safe there aside from the crazy nurse. I was in a psych ward, but it was nothing like what I had seen on television. It was a very nurturing environment. There were no people running around talking to themselves, like in the movies or patients punching themselves. It was just regular people in pain who did not know how to deal with the stress. We played ping pong, checkers, yoga, therapy sessions, art therapy, and more. Unfortunately, we couldn't smoke, and I couldn't wait to get a cigarette.

Once my last day came, they gave me a prescription and told me to follow up with a therapist. I was 90 pounds at the time of my release, so my doctor recommended that I consistently drink Ensure shakes. He also lowered my dosage for the medicine to increase my appetite.

Chapter 16 Pure Survival

My mom said that she wanted me to move in with her. The doctor said it was not a good idea for me to go back to living by myself, so we moved all of my items to my mom's house except for the furniture. I didn't need it. So just like that, no more apartment, no more Pathways to Housing, and my life had changed once again.

The first day I just went into the bedroom and stayed. The next day I was still in bed, and my mom was playing gospel music to inspire me. She played "We Fall Down" by Donnie McClurkin, and the song made me a little emotional. I know she was trying hard to motivate me, so the next day I got up.

She asked, "Is your favorite food still crab legs?" I said yes, and she went out to buy some and came back to steam them. She called me to eat, and I tried hard but barely touched the food. My appetite still had not returned.

My mom had a get together with the entire family a few days later. I hadn't seen some of them in years. They were all being extra nice to me. I knew they were looking at me like damn, she's skinny. In the back of my head I had so much anger and hate for them. Not one person in my family stepped up to lend me a helping hand, a plate of food, or a place to rest my head.

They turned their backs on me. I was a fucking kid who was kicked out of the house to be controlled by sexual deviants and rapists. Man, fuck them! But I had to act as if it was all good, and I was good at hiding my feelings.

I wanted to tell my mom how hurt I was and all the shit I had gone through. How I was forced to use drugs. After the age of 14, I wasn't raised on love. I was raised on pure survival. I thought she would kick me out if I said anything against her, so I counted my blessings and kept those painful thoughts to myself.

My mom cooked up a storm, and I made a plate of food to avoid being judged. I didn't want my family to smile and whisper about me later on. I ate a little bit in the kitchen and threw the rest out while no one was looking. Then I grabbed a chocolate Ensure, which was my favorite.

I was so happy to see my cousins because I hadn't seen them in years. We had a great time talking and laughing. I missed them so much. Maybe living with my mom wouldn't be so bad after all. I got my cousins back.

Everybody started leaving around 10:00 PM, and just like that, they were gone. I didn't see them again for years after that. The next time I saw them was at my grandmother's funeral.

I took my medicine regularly, but my mom said I needed to stop taking it and that I was now fine. So all of my meds were flushed down the toilet. Maybe she was right. All I know is that I had a horrible time getting off the meds. I experienced face tremors and brain shocks.

When I turned my head in certain directions, it would feel like I was being shocked. It took at least three weeks to feel better. I guess things were getting a little better, but I started feeling like more of a burden to my mom. She already had to take time off from work because I blew up one day. I just felt this anger come over me and lost control then threw an iron at the window.

I needed to figure out what to do with my life. However, I had no idea what to do until I kept seeing Army commercials. I told my mom maybe I should join the Army, and she said, "That's a good idea. You could use some structure and discipline." Therefore, I signed up to join the service.

Chapter 17 Sister, Mother, Niece

After my short stint in the U.S. Army, my sister was 19-years-old, and she recently had my first niece, Breanna. Not everyone was supportive of her decision and her relationship. I immediately began thinking of ways to protect my niece. Apparently, my sister also needed protection. My family suspected that her boyfriend was abusing her. The truth came to light shortly after my niece was born. I tried fighting him, but that made nothing better. I was distraught that I couldn't protect my little sister from the evils of the world.

By the time my niece turned two, things were horrible. She was underweight and could barely lift her head. My sister became distant from the family, so the struggles were surprising. My mom brought Breanna a few pairs of shoes. She seemed a bit delayed and only spoke baby jargon. I couldn't go on watching her struggle like that. Therefore, I asked to keep my niece until she got on her feet.

The next day my sister met me at a train station on 34th Street in Manhattan. She handed me the baby with no additional clothes and diapers, but I sympathized with her because I knew she was struggling. We shared a hug I didn't want to end, then parted ways.

I didn't know how long it would take for my sister to come back around, and it was no rush. I had a lot of love to give my niece. After eating, we caught the train to my mother's house. She vowed to help raise her. My first order of action was to get my niece speech therapy. I contacted several agencies, but they told me I needed custody. Thankfully, my sister allowed it, and I officially became a mother.

I could get speech therapy for her in no time once I got custody. Her therapist was a nice woman who came by twice a week, and I watched closely to make sure she tried nothing with my niece. The next problem I had to deal with was her eyes. They didn't develop properly and would move in different directions. She was diagnosed with lazy eyes. I knew how cruel kids could be, and I didn't want her to experience that, so I took her to the eye doctor to correct her problem.

My mom and I put together a well-functioning system for Breanna. I was able to get food stamps, cash, and Medicaid for her. We had a thirty-day follow-up appointment with the judge. He said someone from social services would visit the house to make sure I had a suitable home for my niece.

That same week, the doorman called and said I had a visitor. The professional from Child Protective Services had arrived for our appointment. Shortly after we took a seat in the living room, she told me that the judge granted me full custody, but they needed to verify the living conditions.

My preparation minimized my anxiety. I knew I wasn't doing the best economically, but I had enough to pass the inspection and provide her better care than what she was receiving. When the audit was over, the social worker said, "I am sure you could use some help too." Once I told her I was working, she responded, "Well, Ms. Griffin, you do have the option to place Breanna under foster care for about two weeks. She'd get a nice place to stay, and you'd get a check every month." I told her that wouldn't be suitable, but she remained persistent until it became distasteful.

My niece already didn't have either of her parents raising her, so I knew she faced an uphill battle in life. There is not enough money that could compensate for the stability my niece needed. I wanted to work again, so I followed up on a program at the Veteran's Hospital. A participant could begin with a temporary minimum wage position and then get hired based on performance. It sounded sufficient to me, but I had to wait until my niece could form sentences. I was afraid for her to attend school without being able to voice if someone molested her.

It didn't take long for Breanna to do well in therapy. Once she began talking, she didn't stop, but I loved it. I finally felt comfortable enrolling her in daycare. The system my mother and I had going got even better. We took turns picking her up, and I got the temp position at the VA hospital as a housekeeper. I enjoyed the consistency, but I eventually felt like it was time to get my own place.

I saved up enough money to get a one-bedroom apartment. Even though I wanted my place, I didn't want to move far away from my mother. I found an apartment ten minutes away from her. Getting adjusted to becoming a mother was easier than I expected. All children really need is love, care, and structure. I put locs in her hair, just like mine. My minimum wage was barely enough to pay the bills, so I asked her dad for child support.

Once I took him to court, he did the unthinkable. Her father requested a DNA test to try getting out of paying child support. His stunt prolonged matters by a week. It surprised me that he even showed up at the next court date. However, it wasn't surprising that he was the father. The judge ordered that Breanna's father pay $500 a month for child support. Brian drove me to the courthouse every time and showed the utmost support. After the final appearance, we went to Hooters to celebrate.

My victory was short-lived because Breanna's father skipped town and moved back to Barbados to avoid paying child support. His move was upsetting and triggered my mental health, but shortly overcoming that obstacle signified my growth.

They hired me at the VA Hospital right after the service through a temp program for veterans. It wasn't the coolest job, but it helped me transition out of my mother's place. Being self-sufficient was priceless.

My duties were to clean twelve sick veterans' rooms a day, the hallways, office areas, and make the veteran's beds. It was not easy, but I loved talking to elderly veterans. I met a lot of cool people at the VA and was popular at work.

The newest aspect of my life was dating. The type of girls I attracted surprised most people. Typically, I got attached too quickly and used money to keep women interested. Once it ran out, so did their feelings. Things were smooth at work until my supervisor began making me feel uncomfortable. He started touching my hair and my neck and telling me perverted things. I didn't know how to respond, so I would laugh it off.

The sense of worthlessness crept back in. I felt like that 14-year-old girl again who was incapable of standing up for herself. My supervisor, Mr. White, was a black man, and that furthered my trauma. My other supervisors were no walk in the park, but they never violated me. They were just micromanagers, always hunting their employees down. I began skipping work to avoid Mr. White until I got a warning from the assistant director about my attendance. I didn't want to lose my temp job. My ambitions were to land a full-time position with the company, so I stepped it up at work.

A week after I got my act together, I regained confidence that I would land a full-time position. My spirits lifted, and I began moving at a higher frequency. Usually, I was relatively quiet at work, but I socialized one Friday afternoon during my fifteen-minute break. I was eating cookies and milk while jokes were being passed around by my coworkers. One joke made me spit out my milk. Mr. White, the supervisor, walked up to us after I spit the milk out. He asked me, "What happened? Did I make you cum?" Before I could react, my coworker yelled, "Why are you talking to my sister like that?" Mr. White tried defusing the situation by saying he was only joking, then walked off.

My coworker suggested that I report him to the EEO. I told him no because I thought they would fire me or put me on a different schedule. He volunteered to write a statement, and I took him up on his offer three days later. I gave it to the EEO, and they began putting Mr. White on the night shift periodically.

Somehow the news of the incident spread across the entire staff. That made the situation worse. Because of the backlash, I began calling off work. That was the least of my worries as I began to feel more and more mentally unstable.

My thoughts were racing all over the place, and I started second-guessing my decision.

A week later, I met with the EEO and told them what happened. Then they permanently moved him to night shifts, but unfortunately, we still had to cross paths because our shifts intersected. It pissed off the night staff because all the other employees hated him. Other supervisors began treating me negatively after I stood up for myself against Mr. White. My perseverance paid off. Two weeks later, I got the full-time housekeeping position.

People assumed that I only got the position because the company didn't want me to sue for sexual harassment. Their negative energy dragged me down. I continued working at the VA, but my depression and anxiety got the best of me. I'd miss two weeks of work at a time. My job kept sending me threatening letters that they would fire me, but I barely wanted my life. I had even less of a desire for my employment. I made plans to kill myself on the night I received my third letter from my employer. Shortly after the sunset, I took several pills at once while I cried uncontrollably.

I thought I transitioned to the afterlife until I woke up and began violently throwing up. Even when I woke up, I still assumed I'd pass away in my sleep. Once I made it to the mirror, I didn't realize my reflection. My eyes were extra-wide, and the melanin in my face faded away.

That reflection was what I needed to get myself together. The next day I cleaned up and got ready for work. I kept my head down when I first arrived. My supervisor reassigned me to a different work section when I made it to the break room. My coworkers pestered me about my condition and why I was assigned a different area. During my shift, I ran into my friend Brian. As soon as Brian saw me, he told me I looked like shit, and we broke out in laughter. After he realized that something was really wrong, he asked me to step into his office.

Once Brian closed his door, he said, "So Patrice, what's really up? It looks like you are not eating and depressed." My knees buckled, and I broke down crying in front of him without answering. While I continued crying my eyes out, he asked, "Did you try to kill yourself?" I tried to tell him I did, but I only cried even harder. Then he tried consoling me and told me we needed to go to the ER.

I didn't want to go, but I felt extremely sick, so I complied. They put us in a room shortly after we made it to the emergency room. Before the doctor greeted me, she smiled and said, "It looks like you are struggling a bit." I quickly replied, "I'm not fucking struggling." Her cheerful demeanor died down. Then she responded, "I'm not judging you. We all go through things sometimes." Once the energy in the room calmed down, the doctor asked me several more questions and told me I'd be admitted to the Manhattan VA psych ward. A sedative was in my system before I knew it.

The sedative wore off twenty-four hours later when I woke up in the psych-ward the next day. At that point, I was accustomed to the routine of checking into a facility. When the nurse asked for an emergency contact, I was reluctant to give them my mother's name. My mom threatened that she'd be done with me if I went back to the hospital. Therefore, I gave the nurse Brian's number.

I spent the entire second day trying to figure out how I didn't die yet. It had to be God, although we didn't have a relationship. When I spoke to God, I'd ask, how could he let a pastor's daughter molest me for years and not stop her? Why didn't this almighty God protect me? My cousin preached that homosexuality was wrong but ignored her word and slept with me consistently.

My aunt lived in a mansion, but most of her members were dirt poor and struggled to get by. She was well aware of that, but still preached that they needed to give 10% of their petty earnings to become more blessed by the Lord. Where was God when I was repeatedly raped by grown men and given drugs at such a young age? It felt wrong asking those questions, but it was because of my life experiences.

About an hour after the nurse left, they led me to a conference room with 12 doctors and therapists. One broke the ice and said, "Good morning Ms. Griffin, we at the VA hospital work with a team of doctors that will get you all the help you need to keep you safe. The team and I are happy to have you here. We are going to do all we can to get you back on your feet." Their affirmations came with sympathy. After the professionals asked me several more questions, they vowed to get back with me once they devised a treatment plan.

A group therapy session was next. Eight of us sat in a circle and introduced ourselves, then vented about our pain. Most were abused as children or had PTSD from the war in Iraq. After the session, small talk with the other patients turned into laughs and ping pong games. One of my peers was a 60-year-old Veteran who was also a professional ping pong player who beat all of us before it was time for art therapy. The therapist played classical music, which relaxed my nerves as I painted. They instructed us to paint our emotions. My paintings were dark and depressive.

When lunchtime came around, I didn't have an appetite, but I still had to go to the cafeteria. I sat there pissed while the vets tore up their food. It looked good, but I refused to eat. I hurt myself intentionally because I felt that I didn't deserve happiness or a good life.

I was always the person who would help people, even if it cost me all of my money, food, or possessions. My desire to be liked typically went unfulfilled, and it forced me to suffer the consequences later. I didn't know how to say no. I would say yes, even if I knew I was incapable of making it happen. Then get mad at myself and shut the world off.

Six o'clock that evening, I received my first visitor. Brian was waiting for me in the cafeteria with a big smile on his face. He came bearing gifts and snacks. We spent most of our time joking and sharing priceless laughs. Before our brief visit was over, he gave me $40. Him giving me forty minutes of his time meant the world to me, so I was blown away by his kind financial gesture.

I was once again diagnosed with PTSD and Major Depressive Disorder. They changed my prescription plus added one for anxiety and another for insomnia. I was still experiencing problems, so I took two different medications during the day and one at night. After a week and a half went by, I felt better than ever.

My only side effect was cotton-mouth, and I began getting seven hours of sleep per night. I even packed on five badly needed pounds in a short amount of time. The therapy sessions were productive, and I was ready to continue with my life. My therapist said, "I know you are feeling better, but we must continue monitoring you to make sure you are safe to go home." I assured her I was fine, but I had no chance of convincing her to release me. She sent a letter to my job to inform them I was under a doctor's care.

The staff at the Manhattan VA were excellent and understood my depression and anger. They treated us like family members. Brian visited me every week during my stay and picked me up once they discharged me. The facility gave me my medicine to take with me and set me up with regular therapy appointments at the Brooklyn VA.

Brian took me to Hooters and helped me get re-acclimated. Going to one of my favorite restaurants was a splendid start. The thirty days in the psych-ward felt like three months. I had work at home before work at my job that night. My apartment was a hot mess, but that worked out in my benefit. It kept me busy and distracted me from the loneliness. There were no pictures and no color, just a bed, futon, and a television. My clothes were in a bag, even though I had been living there for two-and-a-half years. I still didn't know how to take care of myself and lived like I was still homeless.

My momentum died down once I made it to work. Before I clocked in for my shift, I began freaking out. I asked Brian, "What if people know and start treating me funny?" He took a deep breath and responded, "I will be honest. Some people know because you weren't yourself. Plus, everyone knows you're a little crazy anyway." Then we laughed, and he continued, "Fuck them. Nobody's perfect, and you will be fine."

Things weren't as awkward as I assumed it would be once I made it to the break room. There were minimal stares, and most people welcomed me back with open arms. They directed me to go to the assistant director, Ms. Gray's office before I began my shift. She wasted little time when I took a seat across from her. Ms. Gray started by asking how I was doing, then said, "I'm glad to see you back on your feet, but you have missed so many days from work that we might have to let you go. I am going to meet with the supervisors today to go over your attendance and whether we will keep you or not." I told her I understood. Then she gave me my keys and assignment for the shift. After Ms. Gray finished, she said, "Try not to curse anyone out or get upset." I expressed confusion about her request, and Ms. Gray stated that she remembered my tangents. Her concern refreshed my memory of something I forgot about.

Brian also reminded me of the past occasions once we crossed paths later that night. He made me feel better about my job being on thin ice. My other colleagues at the VA also helped ease the tension. It was one of the first settings where I was well-liked. I had forgotten about that too.

After lunch, they called me back into Ms. Gray's office. When I made it there, all the supervisors had militant looks on their faces. Apparently, the other supervisors were ready to fire me after looking at my attendance sheet. I was prepared to accept my fate. However, Ms. Gray looked at me deeply in the eyes and said, "It just takes one person to believe in someone to make a change, and I want to give you one. Don't make me feel like I made a mistake." My heart dropped. Then I promised to make her proud while the other supervisors looked pissed.

I knew from that moment that they would be after me, so I couldn't make any mistakes. I agreed to a thirty-day probationary period. The threat of destroying my last chance lit a fire under me to step my game up. Brian served as an accountability partner. He made sure I got up early in the morning and picked me up for work on some days. The other managers provoked me to get in trouble several times, but I didn't fall for it. I finally grew consistent with work, medicine intake, and therapy.

After a while, I became tired of housekeeping, so I started going to college at night. I wasn't sure what I wanted to major in, but I couldn't remain in my profession. There was an in-house opportunity at the VA for a new position in the Engineering department that garnered my interest. The Maintenance Mechanic role paid $21 an hour, but I had no prior experience. A man named Paul, who held the same position I wanted, and John, who was a manager in the department, agreed to teach me and try to help get me on. They never had a female in their department with that title, so my potential accomplishment would be a first. Luckily, I spoke to the hiring manager. I articulated how badly I wanted the position and what I was doing to prepare myself for the opportunity. He told me he'd keep me in mind in case anything opened up.

Two months later, I got the chance I desired. Paul and one of his coworkers gave me a mock interview. They were more supportive than the housekeepers who knew about my potential opportunity in a different department. The mock interview paid off. The director drilled me with questions, but they adequately prepared me. It was a lengthy interview, but I considered that a good sign and was confident after it ended.

One week after the interview, while I was in the cafeteria talking to a couple of guys from the engineering and housekeeping department, I felt someone in my peripheral vision approaching me. Several seconds later, a warm hand touched my shoulder. John, the supervisor I interviewed with for the new position, backed up a few steps once he got my attention. He wore a poker face once I greeted him, and my heart dropped spontaneously. John picked it back up once he informed me that I got the position.

This was the first time my tears signified happiness. Ms. Gray, Brian, John, and Paul seemed to be the only people happy for me. That assumption became apparent once the news broke that I got the position. I was beyond happy to prove Ms. Gray right, who went out on a limb for me. Therefore, I remained unbothered about the hate I received from my other colleagues.

I wouldn't be leaving the housekeeping department for another three weeks, but I secured the promotion. I desired to remain consistent with what was working, so I went to therapy the following week. My therapist spent most of our session being persistent about me continuously taking the medicine. It impressed me that she gave me a safety plan in case things went wrong and warnings about other medications. After leaving, I thought she did not understand that my life was changing, and I didn't need the meds any longer. I finished two weeks' worth of medicine, and I was ready to start my new position.

Chapter 18 I Remember You Sister

The job started off perfectly, and so did my performance. I quickly noticed that there was no such thing as a perfect situation. Some of my new coworkers played games with me, but I didn't stoop to their level. After a while, they stopped, and I became cool with the entire engineering department. One month passed without taking medication or going to therapy.

I felt like I didn't need it anymore until two months went by without taking it. I figured that we all have our good days and bad days. However, I failed to remember that I was not like everyone else. As much as I wanted to feel like a regular person, I had a lot of undealt with trauma. I wanted to believe that I was healed. When you suffer from Major Depressive Disorder, it's like fighting with your mind every day to stay focused and not react to every situation. Being in survivor mode and hypersensitivity to criticism is a time-bomb. It took five suicide attempts to convince myself that I had a mental health problem.

Thankfully, my job understood my challenges. They didn't penalize or stress me when I had to miss a day because of my mental health. I honestly don't know how my coworkers dealt with me because I could barely deal with my up and down emotions. John treated me like a stepdaughter. Even when we butted heads, he remained the bigger person and worked through our challenges. Also, he took me to WNBA games and other events with his family. It felt like a fantasy to have well-rounded consistency.

I finally decided to stay on the medication, but my doctor switched it to something without a bunch of side effects. Plus, I attended therapy twice a week instead of once. I needed to get stable, so I could continue on the right path. The medication was not the answer to all of my problems, but it helped keep me emotionally grounded. My confidence began growing once I became a standout with the company and won several awards.

A work-friend named Kevin stepped up for me during a rough patch. Kevin and I became close, and I looked at him like a big brother even though he was a tad bit flirtatious. I began regretting sharing some personal things with him. It was as if certain men prowled on vulnerability. One night he came by to check on me because I hadn't been to work in a few days. As soon as he came over, I told him I didn't want to live anymore.

He scooted closer to me then said, "Ok, take your pills. I will hold you until you pass out, then call the ambulance for them to call your family." When I asked him was he serious, he said, "Sometimes people just have to go because they can't take the pain anymore. Since I love you, I'm going to do that for you." I didn't say much, but that cut me deeply. He left shortly after that statement, and I became mad that I ignored the red flags. I still had to work with him in the union, but we were rarely alone again.

Two weeks later, a coworker introduced me to a patient during breakfast time at the cafeteria. The elderly black male who was now pale in the face looked familiar. Shortly after small talk, the patient said he knew me from the Black Boots Movement. Then I looked at him as if I locked eyes with a ghost.

While I stood there in silence, he said, "I remember you, sister." I proceeded with caution, but I admitted that I remembered him too. My instincts paid off. After the small talk, he said, "I know what they did to you. You should meet with the elder council, so we can handle that shit in-house. I sharply declined. Then he gave me his number and said,

"Make sure to call me." I rapidly walked away, and it caught my coworker off guard. He tried to get me to come back.

I feared that he would tell the Master Overseer my whereabouts. Thirty seconds after researching the Movement, I learned that Master Overseer passed away, DJ Hotep died of AIDS, and Prince was still living. I began rapidly pacing in circles, then sought my therapist on the 12th floor.

She was on lunch, but I was adamant about seeing her. I broke into sweats while I waited. When I began sweating profusely and uncontrollably, I desperately dashed into the restroom. Once I hid behind a stall, I decided to further my research.

More breaking news was a few clicks away. Willie Lockton passed away also, and they were trying to get a street named after him. It shattered my heart to see a man who caused so much destruction receive that level of praise. I hurried back to the bench to get some air. My therapist came back from lunch at the perfect time because I was only moments away from rock bottom. The breathing techniques and her positive energy rectified my spirits.

Chapter 19 A Battle Every Day

Brian tried encouraging me, but the depression took over again. I stopped eating and bathing. Before I spiraled out of control, Brian took my niece in and cared for her, so she couldn't see how badly I was doing. When I got back on my feet two weeks later, she came back home. I felt guilty, but it was out of my control. Once I left housekeeping and got the engineering job, Breanna was on her way to first grade. Getting off at 4:30 PM put me into a bind. I went to the Board of Education to find other options for Breanna's schooling. They said I could request a variance so that Breanna could go to a school closer to my job. There was one five minutes away. My only concern was that the school only had one other black female. It was predominantly Caucasian and Chinese, but one of the top schools in Brooklyn, so I enrolled her.

Things were going well at her school. In the back of my mind, I always worried about someone touching my niece. I began teaching her about body safety at a young age. Some may deem it overprotective, but my teachings were empowering and protecting her. I wouldn't have been able to live with myself if she experienced what happened to me.

I relapsed less often, but occasionally. Brian and my mom became my support system, but my mom still didn't know what all I went through. She just thought I was tired of raising Breanna, but that wasn't it. I was fed up with my brain fighting against my thoughts and depression. Brian knew what was going on and always jumped in right before I crashed. I hated depression so much, and just wanted to be normal like other people.

The back and forth to different houses, hospitals, and clinics began taking a toll on me. During my fifth year of filling in as my niece's mom, I felt incapable of giving her the home she needed. I told my mom about some of my struggles. Then she came down on me hard for trying to throw in the towel. It was ironic that she felt that way when I put more effort into my niece than what she did with me. No one else was there for my niece, so I kept fighting. I was doing my very best to be a good parent and deal with depression and PTSD. By the time Breanna was in the 5th grade, I regained stability. Things were going great at work, and I had one year remaining to finish my degree.

I saw the light at the end of the tunnel and obtained my Bachelor's Degree in Psychology. Also, I minored in sociology. The thoughts of people calling me a slow learner during my upbringing and still graduating from college gave me the ultimate sense of gratification and the confidence boost I needed.

I was the first of my mother's kids to graduate from college. A few months later, I got sick again, but this time my psychiatrist gave me a leave of absence instead of putting me in the hospital. I battled every day to live a normal life. I won the war because I hurdled over every obstacle to become successful. After ten years of working at the VA, I retired. It was the epitome of bittersweet because I loved my job, but I needed to sacrifice it for my mental health.

Chapter 20 My Voice

Several months after retiring, Breanna and I spontaneously moved to Houston, Texas, for a new start. The warm weather and spaced out environment seemed beneficial for my mental health. I had a lot of love to give, so I got a newborn chihuahua shortly after moving to the Lone Star state. Eight months later, I added on to the family and got another chihuahua.

At the time of my move, my niece was in the 7th grade at a women's college prep academy. I liked the fact that it was an all-girls school that focused on building self-esteem and sisterhood. They had a rose ceremony where all the girls received a rose to let them know that they were beautiful and special.

My niece had a lot of displaced anger because her mom didn't raise her, but she raised her three other sisters. Breanna's pain was very understandable, and I tried to be an outlet for her, but sometimes she took her pain out on me. She even tried putting her hands on me a few times. When Breanna didn't get her way, she would throw herself on the floor like a toddler. I got her some therapy, but I felt uncomfortable with how much medicine they prescribed her.

At first, I was against it because of her age, but then it got out of hand when she became violent towards me and threatened to harm herself. I felt like it was all my fault, but my therapist reassured me she was going through an identity issue. Her friends would talk about their parents, and she didn't have either. All she had was me. I wholeheartedly understood.

Things appeared to get better when Breanna began calling and face timing her mom and sisters consistently. It was only a temporary fix because she started playing her mom against me. Breanna made it seem like I wasn't doing a good job of raising her. She began making up lies about me being a terrible parent. It pissed me off because I sacrificed so many years to take her in when no one else would, and she flipped on me.

My sister and I weren't on good terms because I received no help from her, no birthday cards or care packages, just inconsistent phone calls. That short time that I was supposed to raise her turned into twelve years. I thought things came to a head once Breanna didn't want to go to school or take her medication, but I was sadly mistaken.

One night she ran away, and I panicked and called the police. After I told the officer what happened, his response was, "As hot as it is outside, she will be back." Ten hours later, I got a call from a neighbor. He calmly told me that my niece was lying in front of his door. She laid in the corner of my neighbor's porch as if she were homeless. I told her she could come back after she apologized. My niece remained there until 10:00 PM and gave me a half-assed apology when she returned.

I denied my sister's request for her to return to New York. My mom eventually persuaded me to let her return. I purchased her a plane ticket two weeks in advance before her flight. She didn't talk to me the entire time leading up to her departure, and Breanna left without saying goodbye.

Her departure caused a part of my heart to tear. I walked away feeling confused and had a hard time sleeping the night she left. The following day I broke down in front of my therapist. She said, "You did a great job, Patrice. Your niece was missing something in her life, and that was her mom and sisters. She didn't know how to express herself. Sometimes we hurt the ones that love us the most."

I pretended to be okay with starting my life over without my niece. It took a while to get over my baby being gone. Although I was not her biological mom, I was her mother. I raised her from a baby when she couldn't even talk. Luckily, I had a great therapist. She kept me from crashing and burning. I reluctantly accepted that she was not coming back. I gave away her bedroom set and almost everything that reminded me of her. I had to move forward because she didn't even want to talk to me. She was happy with her family, and I was a non-factor.

Moving into a new place created momentum for moving on. I reached a turning point in 2017. While I was surfing the web, I came across a testimonial that inspired me. A guy named Hassan Campbell said he experienced similar abuse with Afrika Bambaataa, as I did with the Black Boots Movement and Tribe.

Before he came out with his story, I felt as if I lived under a rock, and people would stone me if I spoke my truth. Telling the world about my pain and protecting others from experiencing it felt like a pipe dream until I reached out to Troi "Star" Torain. He previously hosted the "Star and Buck

Wild" show on Hot 97 radio in New York. Just emailing Star about my abuse felt like a victory.

Two days later, I received a bigger victory. He responded and gave me an opportunity to speak my truth on air during a nationally syndicated radio interview. While I spoke, the stress in my body might have taken three years off my life, but it felt like I gained an additional decade after we wrapped up the interview.

Tribe caused me an insurmountable amount of pain for decades, but were never held accountable. I assumed that I would be judged for letting so many years go by without speaking up. People cannot understand that the abuse harms the mind and the spirit more than the body. Staying alive was the priority over speaking up.

It was an insult to injury that they didn't practice what they preached and still received public praise while I was under their spell. I held in all of this pain for years, and Tribe went on with their lives unscathed. The statute of limitations had passed, so I could not file charges, but now I had the power. For some silly reason, I felt they would assume responsibility once I voiced the truth. Instead, they went on a media run to spread lies to protect their image.

I found my voice after the interview with Star and contacted the Special Victims Unit of the NYPD in Brooklyn. The detective I spoke with listened intently and told me to come to Brooklyn to file a formal report. It was surreal when I arrived at the Brooklyn police station during the Dr. King holiday weekend. I must admit, I felt empowered.

Simultaneously, child advocates and survivors who heard my interview reached out to me. The support was unbelievable after feeling so alone and struggling with depression, suicidality, PTSD, amongst other things. They told me their truths, and I had a support system of men and women survivors in America and abroad. It was overwhelming, but in a good way. I made lifelong friends and connected with people that understood me. I felt like an outcast for most of my life, but these new people made me feel like I belonged and have major things to live for.

In 2018, news began circulating about a potential bill called "The Child Victims Act." It extends the statute of limitations for a survivor of child sexual abuse from 23-years-old to 28.

Also, survivors who previously couldn't seek justice through the criminal system would have until the age of 55 to do so. Being that I had to file in New York where the abuse took place, it was necessary to get a lawyer.

I knew it was imperative to align myself with other advocates. Gary Greenberg was one of the first people I connected with. He was a survivor and an active advocate who had been fighting to get this law passed for many years. I joined the fight with Gary and a host of others.

This bill became my number one priority. I reached out to New York's Governor Andrew Cuomo, Senator Brad Hoylman, and Attorney General Tish James via phone calls, emails, and social media. On December 8, 2018, I received a direct message on twitter from a man named Joe Capozzi. He was also a survivor and was putting together a documentary called "A Peleton of One." It would feature a man named Dave Ohimuller, who rode his bike across the United States to support child sexual abuse survivors. Joe wanted to interview me for his film, and it would take place at Senator Brad Hoylman's office in New York. I was appreciative and agreed to take part.

We all continued advocating while Gary organized thirteen rallies to support the bill. The bill gained enough support for the Governor to sign on February 14, 2019. This was a massive victory for survivors in New York, and it sparked a movement in other states to get the same law passed. It exhilarated me that I would finally have my day in court, although I would have preferred them to go to prison for the rest of their lives.

The ruling created some justice, but I desired to do more. A burning passion in my heart ignited the idea for my non-profit organization, "Patrice's Kids." While advocating for the bill, I realized that my ultimate sense of gratitude would come by protecting children from being abused and providing healing for those already victimized. Each person who helped along my journey was God sent. I will forever feel obligated to return the favor to a countless number of others in an infinite amount of ways.

Chapter 21 Unconscious Community

Your mission was supposed to teach the youth about self-love and pride.

Somewhere along the way, you took your awareness and knowledge and flipped it. You manipulated the vulnerable into a state of unconsciousness. You had the opportunity to do good and maybe become a great leader, but you chose evil over good.

You preached about Blackness, but it was really just an excuse to corrupt young minds who needed guidance and love. You spoke about black injustice by the white man, but you were my oppressors.

You said white people hated blacks, but you laid with a white woman every night.

You could have been big brothers, but instead you became my slave masters and my rapists.

You knew all that I had was you.

I was just a kid that loved hip hop and had no direction. Instead of leading me on the right path, you made me spin in a never-ending circle of chaos, sexual abuse, pain, drugs, manipulation, and lies.

You said I was special, but treated me like shit.

You said I was a beautiful sister, but made me feel ugly.

You fooled me. You pushed me into a state of unconsciousness, and I lost myself. I did not understand who I was for years. You said close the crack house, but pushed me into cocaine.

This was not a movement. It was a cult.

You said that your goal was to educate the masses, but you caused destruction.

I'm healing, but this will be forever engraved in my brain.

I will never forget what you did to me.

I will never let you forget what you did to me.

Epilogue

I spent a lot of years being angry, hurt, and feeling abandoned by my mom. There were times I didn't think she loved me. Our relationship was cool sometimes, and other times I felt triggered because my sister got to stay home past the age of 14. She got to travel and have a good life. They moved into a beautiful condo in Brooklyn with a doorman and pool. All I could think was, "What was wrong with me?" and "Why didn't I get the same love?"

I already felt ugly and worthless most days, and there were times I would go a year or two without contacting her. I had a lot of healing to do, and I never wanted to disrespect my mom because you only get one. I kept my distance and stayed in therapy until I could talk to her and share my honest feelings.

My mom retired early and moved to West Palm Beach. We went a few years without talking or seeing each other. I would occasionally send a text to say Happy Birthday or on holidays. Sometimes I'd get sad because I would be in pain and couldn't look to my mom for support and advice or just having her on my side.

I wasn't happy going to other people's homes on Thanksgiving or Christmas. My family celebrated Kwanzaa, but acquaintances were not my family, and I felt more like a charity case than a friend. I just never felt right or fit in.

Deciding to forgive my mom wasn't easy. Perhaps she did the best she could. After all, she was 16 when she got married and was pregnant with me at 17. My dad broke her heart and could have given her HIV. He chose crack and a crackhead over his family.

He left her with three kids, and that must have been tough. I'm just hurt that I got caught in the crossfire. Since January 2020, my mom and I have been working on our relationship. It hasn't been smooth sailing, but at least we can laugh together. I try not to go a day without talking to her.

I hadn't seen my dad in a few years since he never returned from the check-cashing place. My sister called me out of the blue and said, "Daddy is in hospice." I honestly wanted to say I don't give a shit.

For the past few years, I've been acting as if he was dead. It was much easier to feel that way after the way he treated me.

Nevertheless, I went to see him in case he was going to die. I arrived at the hospice, and there he was about 90 pounds looking like death. It was shocking to see him like that.

He had a hole in his stomach and could not eat solid foods. Part of me felt terrible, but the other part felt like if he hadn't cheated on his wife and abused his privilege as a father, he wouldn't have the virus. So, I walked in and said, "Wassup Miles?" They named my brother after him. He responded, "Hey Weedie, how are you doing?" We spoke for a while about his declining health. I came back a few more times to visit, and he asked for money. He even had the nerve to ask me to buy him a beer, even though he had a hole in his stomach. He just didn't quit.

I was moving to Texas, so I told him I wouldn't see him for a while. A year after I moved, my mom called and told me that my dad passed away from complications of AIDS. I flew out to New York, and we buried him a week later. I cried when they put him in the ground, and I never looked back.

When my niece left my home without speaking to me for two weeks and returned to New York, I was angry and hurt. I sacrificed my 20s and 30s for her. I didn't want her to go through anything I had gone through. I treated her as my daughter, not my niece. My job was to keep her safe and give her unconditional love.

We didn't speak for a few months after she moved in with her mom, and when I called, I found out things didn't work out at her mom's house. It didn't even last four months because they couldn't get along. She moved in with another aunt through marriage.

I started to get it. Breanna loves me very much, but all she ever wanted was her mom's love. She was angry and felt abandoned and couldn't understand how her mom had three more kids and didn't raise her. Breanna also went through identity issues because all of her siblings are biracial.

My niece felt lost, which led her to have a poor attitude and act out. She's in therapy now, still struggling with depression, but I believe that in time she will heal. This process may get rough. My sister must recognize that she plays a huge part in how my niece is handling her pain. Breanna is now 18. I will never give up on my niece, no matter how frustrated I get. I just hope that she doesn't give up on herself.

Just six months after moving into my apartment, my grandma's health was on the rapid decline. She had been diagnosed with Alzheimer's disease. The woman that I loved and adored and thought of as the wisest person on the planet had reverted into a childlike state. It was very painful to see her this way. She didn't know any of her kids or her grandkids anymore. My aunts, uncles, and cousins got together at her house to have a meeting to decide on her care arrangements. They decided all of her kids would take turns taking care of her. They gave her the best care possible while her condition deteriorated. Within a year, she passed away at home peacefully in her sleep.

When the Child Victims Act was passed and signed into legislation, it was a monumental victory for survivors in New York City. It would only be civil charges, but we would finally get our voices heard. I was afraid for many years to speak on what happened to me. I would have preferred jail time and the registry for sex offenders, but hey, it was a start. This was the straightforward part.

The hard part was having to find an attorney to take my case. Most of the attorneys were looking for cases involving the Catholic Church, schools, and boy scouts. These cases had the potential to provide lucrative settlements, while suing a broke math tutor wouldn't have a huge payday attached.

I called several attorneys, and they would rush you and say so what happened? As if they were asking you how your day was. It was so uncomfortable. I cried so much, having to tell at least seven attorneys my story over and over. It caused anxiety and triggered me every single time.

I started losing hope until Gary Greenberg linked me with a guy named Matt. Matt is an excellent researcher. He did all the research on my case, and he believed in me. Matt found a loophole that could help my case and get me an attorney. Well, it worked out, and now I have an attorney that believes in me.

My lawyer never treated me like a number. He is compassionate and took his time with me telling my story. There are no guarantees, but now I can seek justice. I got lucky because so many survivors aren't able to seek justice against their abusers because there isn't an institution to sue. We, victim advocates, are working on this very issue.

I dedicate this book to my 14-year-old self. You have been through so much in such a short time. You deserved love, understanding, and protection. Although your life was extremely traumatic and there were times you gave up, you are still here with me.

I'm trying my best to heal that little girl now. I hope you are feeling a little better. I hope you know that I love you. This was never your fault. You can free yourself now because you were always enough. You are beautiful, and you were always worthy of love, and I'm proud of you for sticking in there with me. You will always be here with me.

I would also like to dedicate this book to every single child and survivor who has gone through sexual abuse. I love you, and I understand the struggle even if no one else does. I hope that you can find strength in my story. You may never be able to forget the painful memories, but you can take your power back and start the healing process.

It's a hard journey, but I know you can do it!

www.ingramcontent.com/pod-product-compliance
Lightning Source LLC
Chambersburg PA
CBHW070540170426
43200CB00011B/2496